Praise for *Quantum Marketing*

"*Quantum Marketing* is a masterful guide to navigating marketing's biggest disruption yet. As one of the foremost marketing leaders in the world, Raja offers extraordinary insights and perspectives and pragmatic pathways to pursue. A must-read book for all business executives."
—Keith A. Grossman, President, *Time*

"Raja offers a clear roadmap for marketers to become stronger stewards of brand and growth amid this paradigm shift. Insightful and eye-opening, this is a must-read for any marketer who does not want to become obsolete in today's fast-paced world."
—Michelle Peluso, SVP of Digital Sales and CMO, IBM

"*Quantum Marketing* is a deeply knowledgeable and thought-provoking book, seminal to the times. Raja, as a leading global practitioner of marketing, offers practicable insights to reimagine marketing for the dramatic transformation that is underway. This is a must-read book for all marketing practitioners and students."
—Harris Diamond, Chairman and CEO, McCann WorldGroup

"Raja, who is a cutting-edge marketer, offers not only a fascinating view into the Fifth Paradigm of marketing but also shows how to play deftly in it and win. This is an outstanding book, and it will prove to be a landmark in the world of marketing!"
— Ashok Vaswani, CEO of Consumer Banking and Payments, Barclays

"Raja offers a very different, fresh, and audacious look into the future of marketing. This must-read book makes you realize that it is indeed time to reset the button and take the quantum leap forward."
—Stephan Loerke, CEO, WFA

"For any marketer or business leader, Raja does a great job at preparing us for the future of marketing. A must-read for anyone who wants to be a contemporary leader."
—Pedro Earp, CMO, Anheuser-Busch InBev

"For those looking to embrace, not avoid, the tough questions from their CEOs and CFOs, this book is a must-read. Raja connects the dots for today's quantum marketers looking to unlock brand impact and outcomes in the Fifth Paradigm because, simply put, what got you here won't get you there."
—Wendy Clark, Global CEO, Dentsu International

"In this 'more than a must-read' book, Raja not only presents the critical facets of marketing in the most elegant, eloquent, and clarifying language, but he also helps the reader to truly understand how to harness the powerful force of marketing and its impact for brands and society. *Quantum Marketing* will make you realize marketing can make the impossible into the very possible."
　　—Bob Liodice, CEO, ANA

"The strength of *Quantum Marketing* is in demonstrating how marketers are integral to business success. By exploring marketing's fusion of art, science, and craft, Raja guides marketers to be thoughtful practitioners of their work. It's packed with interesting, practical examples of how to integrate brand building with the data and analytic rigor necessary to drive business growth. An inspiring book full of optimism and hope!"
　　—Leanne Cutts, Group Chief Marketing Officer, HSBC

"*Quantum Marketing* brilliantly describes the tremendous challenges facing future CMOs and how to fundamentally rethink marketing principles and frameworks. A must-read for marketers and business leaders who want to drive growth and thrive in the future."
　　—Ravi Dhar, Professor of Marketing, Yale School of
　　　Management

"In *Quantum Marketing,* Raja provides a clear roadmap for marketers to leapfrog into the future. He peels back the hype and gives pragmatic guidance. An excellent read!"
　　— Zena Arnold Srivatsa, Chief Digital and Marketing Officer,
　　　Kimberley Clark

"Friends, buckle your seatbelts. This, as Raja offers, is an innovative view of the new Quantum Marketer mindset, which is both daunting and yet exhilarating. A must-read for anyone willing to compete for and then succeed in a top marketing job today."
　　—Greg Welch, Spencer Stuart

"One of the greatest marketing leaders of our time, Raja has created this important book to help us prepare for the future of Quantum Marketing. The timing could not be more perfect for this extremely insightful treatise."
　　—Susan Vobejda, CMO, The Trade Desk

"This is the closest anyone could get to spelling out a replicable, successful playbook for the modern marketer in a world where the only con-

stant is change. Raja shares a holistic framework that would help anyone rise to the quantum marketing challenge of tomorrow."
—Anda Gansca, Founder and CEO, Knotch

"Raja, clearly one of the great thought leaders in marketing today, makes a compelling case for a new marketing framework and provides guidance on how to make the most of the opportunities this new environment has to offer. Concise and immensely practical, *Quantum Marketing* is the book to read (and reread) as we head into 2021."
— Gerhard Fourie, Director of Marketing and Brand Strategy, Aston Martin

"Raja's bold and candid observations, mixed with his relentless can-do attitude, is truly a breath of fresh air. This book is a rallying cry for all senior marketers to design and implement a new playbook that will finally acknowledge the power of marketing to drive business growth. Relevant, timely, and actionable!"
—Nikki Mendonça, Global Managing Director of Software and Platforms Industry, Accenture

"*Quantum Marketing* should have a place on every executive's desk and in every business-school classroom. Raja, one of the most influential marketing leaders of our time and a foremost thinker who is a staunch proponent of the purpose imperative, expertly articulates why and how marketers need to 'reinvent their entire approach' for marketing's now and next, and provides a down-to-earth playbook, peppered with colorful anecdotes from his own journey. A must-read for all students of the marketing profession as well as business leaders negotiating the challenges and opportunities of a changing world."
—Jenny Rooney, Communities Director and Chair of the CMO Network, Forbes

"It is rare to find someone like Raja, with such breadth and depth of knowledge, insights and global experiences, so there is no one better to fuse both the art and science of marketing. Anyone trying to transform their business needs to read this book."
—Steven Wolfe Pereira, CEO and Cofounder, Encantos

"Raja is a master of his craft. He brings a new level of depth and dimension to be effective in this ever-changing world. *Quantum Marketing* is the most complete and masterful articulation of what marketing is and how best it should function in the twenty-first century."
—Nick Drake, VP of Global Marketing, Google

"Never before have we seen the fiber of traditional wisdom, modern technology, and a true understanding of the consumer spun together masterfully by a great practitioner of marketing—a must-read for any and all!"
—Pranav Yadav, Founder and CEO, Neuro-Insight US Inc.

"*Quantum Marketing* gives us new frameworks for more scientific and technologically savvy approaches, enabling brands to be connected, relevant, and frictionless across the full consumer experience in the future that lies ahead. A superb book on how marketing can drive more meaningful relationships with consumers!"
—Janet Balis, Marketing Practice Leader, EY Consulting

"Raja's extensive experience as a GM, President, and leading CMO clearly sets this phenomenal marketing leadership resource apart from all others. His insatiable quest in always staying ahead of technology and being able to connect all marketing activities to demonstrate and drive business results are critical skills for every marketing leader today and tomorrow."
—Nadine Dietz, Chief Community Officer, *Adweek*

"In this thought-provoking book, Raja provides a lens into the future of how marketing will continue to evolve and what it would take to be successful. This is a must-read book for every business executive."
—Sunil Gupta, Edward Carter Professor of Business, Harvard Business School

"*Quantum Marketing* displays the thought leadership of a marketing visionary, the practicality of a leading global marketer, and the storytelling of a creative genius. This book will give every practitioner and student the unique vantage point of a marketing guru."
—Devika Bulchandani, President, McCann North America

QUANTUM MARKETING

MASTERING

THE NEW MARKETING MINDSET

for TOMORROW'S CONSUMERS

RAJA RAJAMANNAR

HARPERCOLLINS
LEADERSHIP

AN IMPRINT OF HARPERCOLLINS

Published by HarperCollins Leadership, an imprint of HarperCollins Focus LLC.

Any internet addresses, phone numbers, or company or product information printed in this book are offered as a resource and are not intended in any way to be or to imply an endorsement by HarperCollins Leadership, nor does HarperCollins Leadership vouch for the existence, content, or services of these sites, phone numbers, companies, or products beyond the life of this book.

ISBN 978-1-4002-2403-6 (eBook)
ISBN 978-1-4002-2395-4 (HC)

Library of Congress Control Number: 2020948516

Printed in the United States of America
20 21 22 23 LSC 10 9 8 7 6 5 4 3 2 1

Dedicated to my spiritual guru

Sri Parakala Swamy

Contents

quan·tum

/'kwän(t)əm/
Adjective

1. An extreme, abrupt change . . . as in *quantum* leap or *quantum* change

2. New theories to explain when classical theories break down . . . as in *quantum* physics or *quantum* mechanics

3. New methods and devices that cross existing, known limits . . . as in *quantum* computing or *quantum* computers or *quantum* marketing

quantum marketing
The world is changing with such unprecedented speed and disruption that classical marketing theories, strategies, and practices are failing. *Quantum Marketing* is the new framework for that brave new world of tomorrow. Here, every aspect of classical marketing is challenged and frontline strategies are outlined for marketers to thrive.

Foreword

Executive Chairman, Mastercard

There is one word that comes to mind when I think about marketing these days: *trust.*

Every day in every way, companies must earn the trust of the people we serve. We do that through our products and our workforce, how we support our clients, our partners, and society, and the ways we act and interact at every single touchpoint. Building that trust and reinforcing it—that's what I think about 24/7. How that trust carries over to and is conveyed through a million touchpoints that sometimes don't feel directly connected to us—well, that's what Raja thinks about 24/7.

I have known Raja, professionally and personally, for more than twenty years. In that time, I've seen two forces drive how he approaches his work. The first comes from the fact that he is a marketer who is also a business leader—or a business leader who is also a marketer. No matter how you or I choose to phrase it, the fact is that these two perspectives sit side by side for him and drive a relentless effort to connect brand results to business outcomes. For him, it's not just about goal setting and aligning objectives, it's about actually driving business.

The second is the need to constantly push the boundaries of marketing toward new frontiers. His eyes are always on the horizon of what's coming next—smaller screens, voice-activated assistants, automated cars, you name it—and how that will shift consumer behaviors and how businesses will need to show up in those environments. And, of course, how our presence in these emerging environments can maintain trust and, furthermore, drive business results.

In our time together at Mastercard, I've watched him apply these driving forces in ways that have transformed our marketing as well as the field of marketing in general. And no matter how crazy some of his ideas may have seemed at first mention (dropping our name from the logo, building out multisensory branding, or sponsoring eSports, to name but a few), I've come to find that they are always— always—built on a solid foundation of science and executed with incredible art and consideration. Perhaps that is why Harvard Business School and Yale School of Management have each written case studies based on the work he has led here, and they are now being taught at various management schools around the world.

In my own career, I have seen marketers of all types, and I know what marketers can accomplish for their companies. I have also seen the plight of marketers when they are confronted with hard business questions, as well as their empowerment when they know how to connect the dots between what they do and what the company needs. I, like Raja, believe that massive changes are already underway and the best way to navigate them as marketers who drive business results will be to keep connecting those dots. I also believe this is what Raja offers us here: a way to read the horizon, understand the paradigm shifts, and build out a flexible framework to help us all move forward as trusted brands.

Quantum Marketing is a thought-provoking read for any business executive, whether they consider themselves marketers or not.

Preface

My first experience with marketing was as a young boy growing up in India when I used to go with my mother to the market to buy groceries for the family. We would announce we were "going marketing." For us, the terms *marketing* and *shopping* were interchangeable. The word *marketing* got etched into my mind, and I would associate it with the joys of things to buy, special deals, free samples, fairs and exhibitions, and so on. This was marketing through a young consumer's perspective.

Years later, I was fortunate enough to be accepted into a prestigious graduate school, the Indian Institute of Management in Bangalore. There I began studying "real" marketing, and when I graduated with my MBA, I thought I knew a lot about it. And by the book, I did. So imagine my shock and surprise when I was accosted during the first week on my first job by a director of Asian Paints, the company I joined straight out of college, who asked me: "Raja, we are a market leader already, and we didn't even have a marketing department until now. So, help me understand. What exactly does marketing do?"

It may have been the best business question I've ever heard. And it's among the questions I ask myself often: What role is marketing playing here? What should it be doing? Where is it going? And more importantly, how far can it go?

Currently, marketing is in a crisis. A large number of blue-chip marketing companies are fragmenting the 4 Ps of marketing (price, place, product, and promotion) and distributing them across multiple areas outside of marketing. Without the 4 Ps of marketing, you have to wonder what marketing actually does in these companies. Many of them are cutting marketing budgets year after year, while reducing full-time employees in marketing continually, even laying off entire marketing departments. While brand building is correctly propounded by almost every company as being critical, there seems to be a lurking suspicion amongst C-suite executives that brand marketing is probably fluffy and a wasteful activity that has no immediate impact, if any at all.

In recent studies, 80 percent of CEOs say that they have no confidence in their marketing team,[1] and 73 percent of CEOs said their marketing team members don't have business credibility or the ability to generate growth. Many CEOs don't see value in marketing, or the value that marketing is bringing to the table, and marketers' presence at the CEO table continues to dwindle.

This is an era when marketing executives are capable of affecting business results, both short term and long term, in unprecedented and powerful ways. Yet, ironically, marketing is facing somewhat of a serious existential reckoning.

This crisis of confidence in marketing is the result of three dynamics.

First, we have the big changes in the marketing landscape, driven by huge technology transformation, tremendous advancement in data analytics, and changes in consumer behavior driven by mobile and social media. Collectively, these have shocked business models and upended traditional strategies.

Second, marketers have not been able to credibly connect business outcomes to their marketing investments and actions. Consequently, their contribution and value became increasingly dubious.

Third, too many marketing executives are stuck in a narrow view of what marketing can do and how it can drive the business. At one end, contemporary marketers are linear, analytical, and obsessed with A-B testing, data crunching, and technology deployment. They couldn't care less about the classical, foundational elements of marketing like brand positioning, consumer psychology, or creative finesse. They are focused on performance marketing and the outcomes thereof, but not the "why" behind them. At the other end, you have classical and innovative marketers, who are strong in the traditional areas of marketing, but have no clue about business models, digital technologies, or data analytics. The right mix, and one that has been largely missing, is found in executives who can straddle these two distinct marketing genres, blending the right- and left-brain capabilities, combining creative sensibilities with a command of data and technology.

However, marketing is entering its most exciting inflection point ever, the Fifth Paradigm of Marketing, which I call Quantum Marketing. New technologies like artificial intelligence, augmented reality, 5G connectivity, the Internet of Things, smart speakers, wearables, and blockchains are poised to transform consumers' lives and potentially take marketing's impact to entirely new levels. At this time, the entire function and discipline of marketing can leapfrog toward astonishing levels of consumer insights, real-time interactions, and hyper-targeted, hyper-relevant consumer engagement. Never has the marketing toolbox been more powerful than now. And the ability of marketing to drive business results in the face of brutal competition is not only extraordinary, but vital for a business's future survival.

In the Fifth Paradigm, dramatic new technologies and interaction points will explode into new dimensions. Coupled with that are the sociological changes, marketing ecosystem disruptions, and unprecedented organizational and even existential challenges for marketing. In this kind of a fiery cauldron, companies need a total reboot of marketing to succeed and thrive. That is the button we need to hit and the attitude we need to take as CEOs, CMOs, marketing leaders, teachers, students, start-ups, and everyone else who aspires to succeed in the impending future.

Quantum Marketing is not about forgetting everything we've

ever known about marketing; it's about looking at everything against the backdrop of the fast-paced transformation happening in the marketing landscape and the current slide we are on. It is about seeing and realizing the writing on the wall that marketing—as an art, science, and craft—is indeed in a crisis. It is about reinventing, reimagining, and reinvigorating marketing, to make it an even stronger force that drives the business momentum, i.e., to be a real, demonstrable force multiplier for any business. The Fifth Paradigm will stand many traditional facets and tenets of marketing on their heads. Quantum Marketing is about reframing and reprogramming marketing methods to address and leverage these paradigm shifts.

Quantum Marketing will allow us to understand that this current crisis has its roots in the history of marketing, advertising, and branding, which I detail in this book as various paradigms of marketing. The first two paradigms spanned the early days of print, radio, and TV ads up to the dawn of the internet. The third and fourth paradigms coincided with the internet, Big Data, and the current state of mobile technology, data science domination, and ubiquitous social media platforms. In the Fifth Paradigm, artificial intelligence, augmented reality, virtual and mixed reality, and 5G connectivity will expand marketing into depths and dimensions that can only be imagined.

The Fifth Paradigm will bring about a stunning change in the business of marketing.

The traditional touchstones of marketing will shift rather rapidly. Advertising will continue toward its own existential reckoning. People don't want ads anymore, and, in fact, they are blocking them from their screens with ad blockers and even paying to be in ad-free environments. Loyalty programs will continue to transform, giving way to new paradigms of what it means to keep customers returning to the brand. The competitive landscape will profoundly change as well. It is all uncharted territory—a new and different world—a world of incredible complexity, breadth, scope, impact, and implications. It will also be a world of creativity, innovation, and incredible opportunity. The way a company can leverage marketing to its full potential, and turn it into a business driver and a brand builder, will prove to be a crucial competitive advantage for it. The last five years have seen more change in marketing than the previous fifty. And the next five years will outpace all of them put together. It is both exciting and daunting.

Marketers in particular, and organizations in general, are unprepared for the Fifth Paradigm. At stake is no less than the future of how marketing will exist, what shape it will take, and the context and circumstances under which it will operate. I wrote this book to share my experience as a global marketing executive, to provide a resource to current business leaders, and to serve as both a warning and a promise to the leaders of the future. Unlocking the promise and power of marketing in the future will require a new kind of leadership and a new sense of purpose for its mission. Only companies that can reboot their marketing mission, strategy, and approach will be successful. This book will help you challenge your current thinking and guide you toward mastering the new marketing mindset for tomorrow's consumers.

Welcome to Quantum Marketing!

CHAPTER 1

Marketing's Journey

From Antiquity to Algorithms

Before we begin to understand Quantum Marketing, it is useful to know a bit of history. Because, while we think we've invented everything as modern marketers, the fundamentals of marketing and advertising are thousands of years old. Here's what I mean. Say the name Pompeii and images of people frozen in ash, spouting volcanoes, and ancient treasures come to mind. It is, of course, the site of Mount Vesuvius's eruption in AD 79, and it continues to keep archeologists in work. But these archeologists also discovered something else in the ruins: advertising!

In 2013, a Finnish archeologist found messages about politicians—their personal qualities and policies—written on the houses of wealthy Pompeii citizens.[1] That's advertising, media planning, and location-based targeting at one go!

You will read in future chapters about sonic branding innovations, where brand identities are created using sound. Documents from ancient China detail a practice of candymakers playing a bamboo flute to attract customers.[2] And while we look at banner ads as a clever invention, an ad for needles, dating to the Song dynasty (960–1279 CE), says, "We buy high quality steel rods and make fine quality needles that are ready for use at home in no time." The advertisement also contained the image of a rabbit holding a needle, a mascot for the brand or a precursor to a logo.[3]

From those simple beginnings, marketing has never stopped evolving. From antiquity, the biggest leap in marketing was with the advent of the printing press in the fifteenth century. Ads started appearing in magazines and posters. Product packaging advanced to convey quality and benefits. The nineteenth century saw the birth of ad agencies and ads for soaps. Then came along radio, newspapers, TV, cable, internet, and the torrent of digital marketing. Even in the very early forms of marketing, it is fascinating to see the modern concepts of location-based ads, social media, and marketing measurement, in whatever rudimentary form, baked into the human instinct to influence the thinking, emotions, and behaviors of people and societies. There has always been a dominant approach in each phase, but the phases are not exclusively linear. For example, you will find defining features of Pompeii's approach (such as using high-traffic locations) in Burger King's app and its geolocation-based marketing in 2020, in which it cheekily feeds special offers when a customer is in the proximity of a McDonald's.[4] And you will find the basic product logic that defined the early days of print advertising prevalent even today across multiple brands.

THE FIRST PARADIGM:
THE PREMISE OF LOGIC AND RATIONALE

The First Paradigm of marketing was literal, rational, and almost entirely product centric. The presumption was that consumers made their purchase decisions rationally and logically. If you produced the best product, the thinking was that consumers would flock to it. So, marketers had a defined purpose and a simple strategy:

Make your product better than your competitors'. And let the consumers know about it. Marketing connected the product to the consumer by creating and leveraging a product's feature set that was different from and better than the competition or by offering the product at a lower price. Tide "got clothes cleaner." Dodge cars had a "smoother ride."[5] And for vacuum cleaners, "Nothing Sucks Like Electrolux."

The advent of mass production created a level of product parity and commoditization. Every brand's research and development focused on superiority in product quality, which resulted in marginal differentiation and minimal competitive advantage at best. At this point marketing started to highlight, and even exaggerate, feature sets that mattered to the consumers. And to top it off, marketers had credible or credible-looking people endorse the brands to make consumers believe the claims. Doctors endorsed the health safety of Lucky Strikes.[6] This, of course, was the beginning of the erosion of trust between consumers and brands, and advertisements slowly began losing credibility. This also marked the beginning of advertisements affecting and shaping culture, including, unfortunately, the stereotyping of gender.

THE SECOND PARADIGM:
IT IS ALL ABOUT EMOTIONS

Marketers, over time, realized something very powerful: people make decisions emotionally, more than rationally or logically. In fact, in many cases, entirely emotionally! Therefore, they began incorporating emotions into their ad campaigns. When TV came on the scene, it brought visual and audio together into a powerful new medium through which stories could be told very compellingly. Interestingly, emotional claims needed no scientific or data-backed proof. This, when stretched a bit, was euphemistically referred to as creative freedom or flexibility. With the trend toward engaging emotions, marketing became an invitation to an experience, more than just a push to buy the product.

Companies and brands took their focus on product appeal to a whole new level. The focus on ingredients and product performance in the First Paradigm was supplemented, or even replaced, by an emotional promise. Relationships, affinity, status, attractiveness, happiness, joy, success—all of these became mythical qualities that the consumer could attain like the membership benefits in a secret club. Think Coca-Cola and their promise that "Things go better with Coke," or Pepsi as the soft drink for a New Generation.

Marketing mined emotions. Brands and companies began creating emotional spaces and then occupying those spaces. While a product feature set could be matched or bettered, and therefore the product could be dislodged from its market position, emotions were much tougher to compete against. Once a brand occupied an emotional territory, it pretty much owned that territory for good. Almost.

But how do you market on emotion? Associating your brand with esoteric qualities, whether luxury, indulgence, freedom, or status, became a competitive strategy. Understanding and improving the product was still necessary. But now companies and brands set out to understand consumer mind-sets, motivations, attitudes, and behavior. Companies launched attitudinal metrics, usage and habits studies, focus groups, and psychographic research.

As marketers learned more about what consumers aspired to, who their role models were, and so on, they started to lean more on celebrities as a way to create emotional connections and aspirational pathways. The stars of the Second Paradigm were not just an anonymous Coppertone Girl or the generic doctor who endorsed cigarettes. The stars of the Second Paradigm became the face of the product. Brooke Shields was Calvin Klein's. Madonna was Pepsi's. Michael Jordan was Nike's. Advertising had a clear task. Marketing had a clear approach.

THE THIRD PARADIGM:
THE INTERNET, DIGITAL MEDIA, AND DATA

Marketers were coasting along leveraging emotion and identity to reach consumers who were becoming obsessed with both of those things. But something was sneaking up on them. On August 6, 1991, an arcane information retrieval system known only to scientists was shared with the general public by Tim Berners-Lee. It was called WorldWideWeb. There was no press release. To paraphrase W. B. Yeats, a "terrible beauty" was born.

Four years later, this terrible beauty started to be monetized. On October 12, 1994, a digital trade information website called Hot-Wired simultaneously published ads from twelve different brands, including AT&T, MCI, Volvo, Club Med, 1-800-Collect, Sprint, and IBM. Banner ads were created.[7] Digital marketing was born, and everything about marketing, advertising, and media changed in an instant. It was the exact moment at which speed, scale, and impact was born and nothing about marketing has been the same since.

This was the entry into the Third Paradigm: the rise of the internet and data-based marketing. After TV, it was the next major technological disruption of marketing. Data, which was previously restricted to the techies, geeks, economists, researchers, and the like, found a new patron. Marketers discovered the power of data, and they saw the jump in effectiveness it could produce. The new focus became using data to create more targeted marketing, which minimized waste, stretched the dollar, and vastly improved a company's ROI. This paradigm saw the rise of data scientists and data-savvy marketers in the commercial world. With the internet, marketers now had an extraordinary ability to reach, communicate to, and impress their prospects and customers as never before—at scale, with economy and precision.

But not everything was digital. The Third Paradigm also saw a dramatic increase in direct mail, direct response advertising, and the promise of the "segment of one." In other words, every consumer was recognized and treated as unique, and highly individualized marketing messages could be conveyed to them in customized, memorable, and impactful ways. Direct mail offers by companies like Citibank, which started as a tool to drive customers to consolidate their credit card balances, were advanced into the data-driven era of personalization. Marketers improved their targeting in the Third Paradigm so much so that consumers warned marketers about getting too close and too invasive. This resulted in consumer advocates calling for regulators to pass rules in 2003 that mandated companies to abide by the Do Not Call or Do Not Mail lists in the US.

If direct marketing got close to consumers, the internet entered their DNA, figuratively speaking. Marketers' email or messaging prowess brought them within arm's reach of the consumer. When a consumer searched for a product, the internet came back with that information, which in turn gave the marketer insight into consumer behavior as never before—and the chance, therefore, to get even closer. And marketers were willing to pay for these opportunities. For this reason, web browsers like Netscape, Excite, and Yahoo were the first profitable internet businesses. It was only when Google came in with AdWords that profitability took on a whole new meaning. In fact, as early as 2000, Harvard Business School professor John Deighton described the internet as a multidimensional "total environment for doing marketing."[8]

Consumers, too, were empowered by the internet. They searched for products, searched for one another, and found they wanted more of everything. The internet and the data it generated was the combination of technology and platform that gave the Third Paradigm a stage. And yes, it was a huge inflection point. Every visit, click, and page view generated precious data on consumer behavior, preferences, and spending patterns. The explosion of internet advertising very quickly showed how attractive data was. The first year that marketers began to think of the web as an advertising medium was 1997, when internet advertisers in the United States spent $940 million, and it spiked to $4 billion in 1999.[9]

The comfort level marketers (sort of) had with not being held accountable for ad effectiveness changed, for the most part, with the advent of data. Data transformed advertising measurement, removing guesswork and audience estimates. Did an ad work? TV ratings were no longer the answer. Did a newspaper ad drive sales? Circulation statements were no longer relevant. An advertisement was successful if people saw it and acted on it. Both these actions were suddenly measurable in the new internet era and were measured to fractional detail. Was a particular media worth advertising on? That answer was defined by the number of viewers who matched the target profile and interacted with it every day. Data so defined the business media that placements were surgical.

Then enters the phrase *real time*. Real-time activity—a consumer's immediate past actions or current location—could lead to a customized offer or communication with that person. It moved true one-to-one marketing toward reality. Marketing ROI was now defined with precision. For the first time, marketers could reliably measure responses driven by different marketing strategies and tactics. The traditional purchase funnel (Awareness => Interest => Desire => Action) was now being reevaluated as marketers developed more sophisticated purchase models. Traditional goals like raising brand awareness and establishing competitive superiority were matched with driving purchase consideration and purchase intent. The art of marketing melded with the science of marketing. These changes also created demand for a new kind of marketing executive. The "Mad Men" who lived on big personalities and big perks had to change or change jobs. Data savvy became a prerequisite for a marketing executive.

In the Third Paradigm, data evolved into an enabling engine. Data provided the consumer with utility, dynamic frames of reference, and a sense of overall personalization. For the marketer, it provided ways to calculate and understand the value of the consumer over his/her lifetime to the company, i.e., lifetime values. They were also able to arrive at more accurate retention models. Data became a competitive advantage. The competitive drive from the 4 Ps of marketing famously postulated by Philip Kotler had come full circle. Now data could join the 4 Ps as a key pillar of the competitive strategy.

THE FOURTH PARADIGM: ALWAYS ON

The internet was hardly being digested when two new dimensions were being created, both of which would come to define the Fourth Paradigm. From October 2007 to August 2008, a college-based variation on message boards called Facebook spiked from fifty to a hundred million users, and social media was born. Alongside this, the iPhone was released on June 29, 2007. Mobile phones and mobile devices totally altered the consumer landscape once and for all. The mobile phone virtually became an extension of the human body, with consumers going to bed and waking up with it. Now, marketers had a medium available through which they reached consumers anytime.

Forces Leading Up to the Fourth Paradigm

Four foundational elements led to the birth of mobile phones and devices: Exponential increases in processing power, miniaturization of components and devices, all-pervasiveness of an affordable internet, and a big leap in user interfaces that became highly intuitive. With their ubiquity and together with another revolution—social media platforms—everything in the consumer landscape got transformed. This is Paradigm Four.

Figure 1 shows six disruptive dynamics leading to the Fourth Paradigm. The sheer scale at which consumers consume content is nothing short of staggering. In a single moment, eighteen million people around the world send a text via phone apps. Four million

YouTube videos will be watched. One million people will log into Facebook. Forty-one million people will send a message on Facebook Messenger or WeChat. Four million people will enter a search query on Google.[10] These humongous and disruptive dynamics have wrought enormous changes to the consumer landscape.

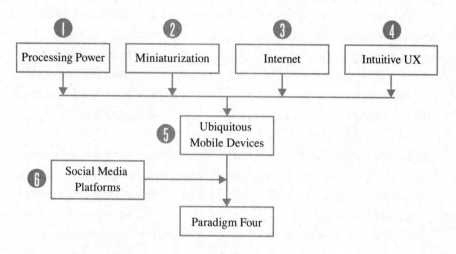

FIGURE 1

Consider the following:

➤ **Always on and always distracted:** The average human attention span is less than eight seconds, driven down to the level of a goldfish by the constant stimuli of the Fourth Paradigm. People check their phones an average of eighty times a day while on vacation, with some checking their screen more than three hundred times each day. People are spending upwards of six hours a day on different digital devices.[11] And consumers are being bombarded by an average of five thousand commercial messages every day. They are learning to tune them out, so they barely even notice these commercial messages coming at them.

➤ **No time for prime time:** In the good old days, we used to talk about prime time. This is the time when the whole family would gather around the TV and watch a popular program on a given channel. As a marketer, one knew exactly which programs and channels to place ads in, to reach the right audience. Now, with each individual having multiple devices, they are using them to view a lot of video content. They view what they want—typically alone, not as a family—when they want, on demand. No more prime time. The viewership got hugely fragmented. Now it takes much more mathematical heavy lifting to plan for a reliable and quality viewership. It involves a tremendous amount of quantitative modeling to make sense out of the chaos and act on it to drive reach and results.

➤ **Social media heaven and hell:** The reputation and even the valuation of a company can be made or broken by a single tweet in the Fourth Paradigm. The Ellen DeGeneres selfie of Bradley Cooper, Jennifer Lawrence, and other stars at the 2014 Oscars was taken with a Samsung phone and it was retweeted two million times in two hours.[12] Here's hell: Kylie Jenner made headlines in early 2018 by firing off one tweet: "Does anyone use Snapchat anymore?" That set off a downward spiral for Snap's stock ($SNAP). A headline from CNN Money read: "Snapchat stock loses $1.3 billion after Kylie Jenner tweet."[13]

TRANSCENDING SCALE

There are now more mobile devices than there are people on the planet. As a result, businesses have an opportunity to target and connect with consumers in real time, across geographies, in radically more efficient methods. The power and ubiquity of devices has transcended generations, geographies, and cultures.

The Fourth Paradigm emphasized the science over the art of marketing. Media planning has been automated, driven by click rates, page views, and content adjacencies. Programmatic advertising, dependent on algorithms and complex bidding schemes that rival any stock exchange, have become dominant. More than 65 percent of digital advertising in 2019 was estimated to have been purchased and served by an algorithm.[14] Releasing an advertisement into this programmatic environment requires a new method for measuring whether an ad was viewed, whether it was viewed by a human or a bot, and how much it should eventually cost.

Measuring digital advertising performance has become so complicated that hundreds of entities, including ad technology and marketing technology companies, sprung up, thrived, and have been purchased for huge multiples in this space. The ad ecosystem is so complex now that it needs a ton of players just to help make sense out of it and keep it going. It has been estimated that these various intermediaries get 40 percent of all the ad budgets.[15]

But not all is well as a result of Fourth Paradigm changes. A trust problem has ensued with the advertising ecosystem, both from marketers and consumers. Much of that was highlighted by a K2 Intelligence report that found rampant kickbacks and unnecessary markups from agencies, ranging from 30 percent to 90 percent of client spend. "Media buyers were sometimes pressured or incentivized by their agency holding companies to direct client spend to this media, regardless of whether such purchases were in the clients' best interests," according to the report.[16] The US Department of Justice has launched an investigation into this whole murky business.[17]

Apart from the trust issue between clients, publishers, and agencies, there is also a trust problem from consumers' point of view. They are rightly concerned about their data privacy, and that concern has gained enough momentum that it has spawned strict regulations. The EU instituted the General Data Protection Regulations in 2018. Among other things, it requires all companies to clearly state the purpose of the data they are collecting, get specific permission from consumers to opt in, to data collection, and allow consumers to delete their information at any time. A similar law has been enacted in California in early 2020.[18] Many countries and regions around the world are looking at this issue seriously.

TO SUMMARIZE . . .

We've moved through four paradigms of marketing. The First Paradigm was driven by the product as hero, based on the simple premise that consumers make logical purchasing decisions. The Second Paradigm delved into the emotional realms of consumers. It was largely a reaction to the difficulty of attaining differentiation purely based on product functions and benefits. And many times, the emotion itself was doing the job, even to the conspicuous absence of the product. The Third Paradigm was the era of internet and data-driven marketing. Data analytics brought in a new layer of understanding and depth to marketing that spanned all the way from digital targeting to new campaign measurement metrics to calculating lifetime customer relationship values. And the internet was the platform that allowed marketers to understand consumer interests and intentions, serving them with the right messages economically. The Fourth Paradigm ushered in mobility via digital devices, which have literally become extensions of the human body and obsessions of the human mind. Mobile and real-time location technologies as well as social media platforms ushered in the era of the connected consumer. Marketers followed along digital channels and social networks.

We've come a long way from the walls of Pompeii and the needles of the Song dynasty!

CHAPTER 2

The Fifth Paradigm

Now we stand at the precipice of the Fifth Paradigm. This is the era of Quantum Marketing (see Figure 2).

THE FIVE PARADIGMS OF MARKETING

Paradigm One	Paradigm Two	Paradigm Three	Paradigm Four	Paradigm Five
Product Marketing	Emotional Marketing	Data-Driven Marketing	Digital & Social Marketing	Quantum Marketing

FIGURE 2

This era is driven by exponential disruptions (good and bad) in consumers' lives, caused by a deluge of emerging technologies. And the resulting changes in the consumer landscape call for marketers to tap into the dynamics of the new paradigm and reinvent their entire approach. It is a time when mistakes are exponentially magnified and success is as fleeting as the consumer attention span. In general scientific terms, "quantum" describes an effect that cannot be explained by classical approaches. It has also come to mean an unmeasurable jump in speed or volume. Both of these describe marketing in the Fifth Paradigm—Quantum Marketing.

First, let's look at the incredible, emerging landscape.

➤ **Infinite data.** Sensors of all types have begun taking root in consumers' lives from the Internet of Things (connected refrigerators, washing machines, dishwashers, home thermostats, and so on) to wearables (smart watches, smart rings, smart fitness trackers) to smart speakers and digital assistants and connected cars. These sensors capture unprecedented levels of data from literally every breath, move, feeling, and action of consumers. If marketers know how to use this quantum data explosion, they can gain incredible insights that will propel the effectiveness of their campaigns and consumer engagement to extraordinary levels. I will elaborate with examples in the following chapters.

➤ **Artificial intelligence (AI).** I have dedicated an entire chapter to AI because it is the big difference maker. Whatever you do with data currently, from simple consumer surveys to complex predictive analytics, AI will make it look like child's play. AI can look at the endless troves of data of all kinds from a multitude of sources and make sense out of them and generate powerful, actionable insights as never before. And the best part is that these insights will be available in real time, so actions can be taken with zero or near-zero lag, for maximum impact. And the impact itself can be measured in real time, so optimization can also happen in real time. That's Quantum Marketing. On another level, AI will totally disrupt the creation of content, not just by supplementing existing resources and processes but by even supplanting them, with enormous power and speed. AI will let marketers have a finger on the pulse of everything that is going on at every stage of the marketing life cycle, make sense out of it, and act on it for highly effective outcomes.

➤ **Blockchain.** Today, there are a ton of middlemen across the marketing value chain. A value chain is meant to be a sequence of processes or activities that add value at every stage. The presence of these middlemen is, in many cases, needed because of a lack of transparency and trust between the marketers who are paying the bills and their counterparties. For example, if a marketer is putting out an ad in the digital space, they need to know if the ad was actually served, if it was properly viewable, if it was viewed by human beings, and so on. To verify all this, there are various ad tech and other companies that came about and proliferated. And they all need to be paid. This means that some of the marketing dollars, which would have otherwise gone to working media, would be funding these middlemen. Blockchain will alleviate this issue. The unnecessary intermediaries will more or less vanish. There will be direct digital contracts between advertisers and publishers that will be untamperable and updated automatically based on how, when, and where the ads are appearing and in what form. Additionally, blockchains will also help with establishing the authenticity of products, to combat fakes and imitations.

➤ **5G.** For marketers, 5G will be the difference between a tricycle and a motorcycle. This is a radically powerful telecommunications protocol that will fuel the functioning of other technologies such as the Internet of Things, autonomous and connected vehicles, live holographic projections, and mixed reality. It will have a profound impact on marketers. For the first time, marketers will be able to deploy immersive virtual reality or 3-D experiences around their products and services remotely and in real time. They will be able to capture and process signals from consumers' sensors and actions, analyze and deploy appropriate tactics on the go, as they happen. A number of other emerging technologies will be enabled by the presence of 5G networks.

OTHER EMERGING TECHNOLOGIES

➤ **Augmented reality.** AR will be one of the technologies that adds a new dimension to the marketer's tool kit. It will enable marketers to add additional layers of information into the physical or virtual environments, to vastly improve consumer experience. For example, if I am walking on a street and pull up my phone, on the screen I can see the street ahead but also see virtual flags or banners that show where there is a coffee shop, where there are special offers, or where my Mastercard gives me Priceless Experiences. This will take consumer engagement to a different level.

➤ **Virtual reality.** From a two-dimensional screen to 3-D formats, the quest has always been to give consumers immersive experiences, to make them lifelike and highly compelling. With the advent of VR-enabled, wireless spectacles and headsets, VR will add an entirely new dimension to content that can provide new options to brands for messaging and sponsorships. And what's more, enabled by 5G, marketers will be able to reach consumers in real time, in a contextually appropriate fashion. For example, if a travel company is trying to market a destination to the consumers, it can transmit any VR video of a given destination that the consumers seem to be interested in, instantly, so the consumer will have an immersive experience and appreciation of what is in store in that destination. The impact on consumers will be manifold compared to what it would be when they see a regular video of that destination, which in itself will be manifold of the impact of seeing just the pictures of that destination. Sales and conversion rates will be far higher, as a result.

➤ **3-D printing.** 3-D printing technology is in a relatively nascent stage, and 3-D printers are evolving, making them cheaper, faster, and more versatile. The applications for 3-D printing are spreading across many fields. 3-D printing will enable things to be printed on-site, as opposed to being shipped from elsewhere, which can transform the supply/distribution chain. 3-D printing also enables rapid prototype development. For marketers that will mean rapid-fire testing and a true Quantum Marketing approach.

➤ **Connected and autonomous cars.** These are already being rolled out as we speak. In autonomous cars, consumers will have more time to pay attention to things other than driving, and they will be seeking to fill that time with content they care about. If you are a fast-food company, you want to make sure that you are in front of consumers when they have an impulsive moment. If you are a credit card company, you want to be the payment vehicle at that time. If you are a media company, you want to capture the consumer's visual and audio attention while they're in the car. The autonomous car will be a mobile living room or a mobile office when combined with 5G and other technologies. That opens a slew of possibilities for marketers.

➤ **The Internet of Things (IoT).** Almost every appliance is being connected to the internet. And, as Mastercard famously said, "Every connected device is a commerce device." I would go a step further and say, "Every connected device is a marketing device." Soon consumers will be able to talk to their fridge, washing machine, dishwasher, thermostat, and so on, and it will talk back. These represent new media for marketers to play with and use to reach consumers in a highly contextualized fashion.

➤ **Smart speakers.** While smart speakers can be technically classified amongst IoT, they deserve a distinct look, given how fast they are proliferating. Google Home, Alexa, and others have already penetrated 25 percent of US households. Consumers interact with them via their voice—from searching, querying, setting alarms and reminders, seeking information and entertainment, all the way to making purchases. These smart speakers totally disrupt the current purchase funnel. And because there is no visual real estate, marketers need to figure out how their brands show up in a nonvisual environment. Mastercard has done some pioneering work in the area of sonic branding, and we will cover more of this shortly.

➤ **Wearables.** Wearables are developing in a multitude of ways. To name a few, they track health vital signs, remind you to stand up, and even measure your moods, making wearables effective data-gathering and communication tools for marketers. It is a completely different ecosystem, with its own standards and nuances. Like for IoT, there is a whole new opportunity for players to pull the ecosystem standards together and enable marketers and consumers to interact effectively and efficiently.

➤ **Robotics and drones.** Both in industrial and consumer settings, robotics and drones can bring substantial disruption. Already several hotels, in the United States and in various international markets, have robots doing room service or delivering toiletries and other knickknacks to the rooms. This is spreading pretty fast, with hotels like Aloft, Hilton, and Crowne Plaza all investing in robotic services and deploying robots already. KFC has deployed robotic waiters at restaurants in Japan. Amazon is on the verge of delivering packages by drones,[1] as is UPS. These two technologies can have a profound impact on the distribution and logistics space in short order, helping marketers gain significant efficiencies in the fourth P (place, that is, distribution).

Other than the technological disruptions we just walked through, there will also be some profound sociological and systemic changes that will disrupt the marketing ecosystem and practices. As a result, most of the classical approaches will break down. I will cover these in depth in the coming chapters.

Here are some of those:

➤ The concept of loyalty will be completely transformed. New concepts that accept the undisputable truth about how consumers really see their relationships will come to the fore.

➤ Advertising will radically change. Concepts like Quantum Experiential Marketing will emerge, to address and connect with the hyperconnected consumer.

➤ Agencies will be disrupted. In fact, the entire ad ecosystem will transform, where traditional lines blur and new business models will emerge.

➤ Marketing will be fragmented. Given the extensive complexity of the field and the relative lack of understanding outside of marketing on the role it plays and can play, the function will get fragmented, before it comes back together.

➤ Purpose will become an indispensable part of marketing. Purpose will move from being a politically correct stance of companies into an essential North Star that guides the company and is brought to life by marketing.

➤ Ethics and values will gain significant prominence. Trust will be a gigantic competitive advantage. Ethics and values will be at the root of building and sustaining trust.

➤ Crises will happen more often and risk management will become critical. Marketing will be at the center of both crisis events and crisis resolution. Risk management will become a key tenet of marketing.

TO SUMMARIZE . . .

The Fifth Paradigm will feel like a whole new planet for marketers. Crazy new technologies, an extraordinary quantum of data, fleeting life moments becoming accessible, an opportunity or threat of real-time actions, the collapse of the purchase funnels and other classical theories and frameworks—all of these will totally alter the marketing landscape, and marketers will have to reimagine their strategies, structures, and talent.

In the Fifth Paradigm, brands will create excitement, engagement, and inspiration for their products and services using new technologies, new media, new frameworks, and new insights. Consumers will expect not only great products and experiences, but they will demand marketers use all the resources available to make a positive difference to society, either by helping it be more just and equitable or for the planet to become more sustainable. The key factors that determine success are: authenticity, immersive interactions and experiences, real-time marketing, sensible and sensitive marketing through the consumer life cycle, and remote delivery and management of everything from the more obvious logistics to experiences to product demos to training and development of the marketing teams to learn and stay at the cutting edge of the fields that impact marketing.

To survive and thrive in the Fifth Paradigm, marketers will need open-mindedness and technological savvy. Marketers will need to master their grasp of technologies and their applications as spelled out in the following pages. If they don't, they will most likely be among the casualties mentioned in the preface.

For the consumer, the Fifth Paradigm will be a labyrinth of content, messaging, imaging, new devices, and automation, all happening at new levels of intensity and complexity. As any marketing executive—or student, for that matter—will know, marketing must meet the consumer, now and forever. That intersection will be crowded and noisy. That intersection is the Fifth Paradigm.

CHAPTER 3

Reset the Mission of Marketing

The intersection where marketing meets the consumer in the Fifth Paradigm will be extraordinary in its activity. Any marketer who thinks they can simply drive into that junction without the proper command of new technologies and data analytics is deluding themselves. But even with that knowledge in hand, there's another critical task for the new journey. That is one of resetting the mission and role of marketing. I will cover the mission reset in this chapter and go into data, technologies, and sciences in the following chapters.

When I graduated from the Indian Institute of Management in Bangalore, India, more than three decades back, marketing was a top choice for graduates. It was seen as a hip, excellent career path that offered a strong growth trajectory, a lot of creativity, and opportunities to see innovation in action. It was a highly visible function that had a significant impact on business.

It also offered very lucrative financial rewards and a great opportunity to travel. It involved leveraging both the right brain and the left brain. In fact, marketing was probably the only field where an ambitious young person could skillfully integrate their creative and analytical prowess and see their ideas take shape in the market-place right before their eyes. It was a heady experience! No wonder marketing was the top choice for most top students in those days.

But something happened over the last three decades. Marketing somehow seems to have lost some of its gravitas, glory, glamour, and glitz.

Many companies are fragmenting and reducing the role of marketing. These are not some obscure, industrial brands or companies in obscure industries. These are reputed Consumer Packaged Goods (CPG) companies. Coca-Cola even eliminated the role of CMO (but thankfully brought it back as the need was clearly felt).

Let's ask ourselves why the 4 Ps of marketing—product, price, place, and promotion—are increasingly being parsed out to areas outside of marketing to manage. For the last several decades, marketing was personified by the confluence of those 4 Ps, thanks to Philip Kotler's seminal work. Today, there are any number of companies in which marketing does not manage product, does not manage pricing, does not manage place (distribution). It just barely hangs on to promotions, which is advertising and promotions at best. Take away all these functions from marketing, and it is legitimate to ask ourselves, what the hell does marketing do, then?

This is not uncommon. In speaking with a number of CMOs from around the world, I see that this has been an increasing trend over the last few years, particularly over the last ten. So, what happened?

First, there has been an explosion of mobile technology, the saturation of internet penetration, the social media tsunami. In other words, The Fourth Paradigm of Marketing was happening. Marketers have not been able to keep pace with the dramatic advancements in technology and data. CMOs have typically been biased toward the creative side of the house, and they were more at home in the creative aspects of their role than in the analytical and quantitative aspects. Hence, there has been phenomenal progress in marketing's artistic, aesthetic, and design elements. This served companies and their marketing departments quite well, till the time data and technology started coming at marketers like a flood. Traditionally, marketers have not been very tech savvy, and they have not been known to be very data savvy either.

Classical marketers were quickly overtaken by a new breed of technologists who dove deeply into marketing and saw opportunities wide open, unexploited, and underleveraged. Real digital marketing was born and started setting the pace, processes, and methodologies completely outside of marketers' purview. A sharp divide opened between two breeds of marketers. On one side stood the classical marketers, more familiar with the 4 Ps, positioning, the purchase funnel, and all the finer and fundamental aspects of marketing. And on the other side stood the new breed of contemporary marketers, who have very different skill sets. They're all about data, technology, experimentation and testing, and highly automated and programmatic operations. They couldn't care less about the foundational aspects of marketing.

Even today, if you were to ask many traditional marketers to explain exactly what happens inside programmatic ad technology, or what happens inside a particular kind of digital technology, they may at best be aware of it superficially. Dive a little deeper and they are totally lost. They are not in command. They're completely at the mercy of the third parties or others who are savvier in this space.

NEXT UP: THE DATA WAVE

The other wave that broke was about data and data analytics. Again, since marketers and CMOs have not come from that side of the house, many of them lack an understanding of and command over data analytics. They are quite frazzled when someone throws a lot of data at them. In this day and age, if marketers don't know how to maneuver data, how to leverage data, how to navigate data analytics, they run the risk of becoming obsolete and irrelevant.

There is a third angle to this whole phenomenon of marketing losing its seat at the table. With the advent of social media, there has been an unprecedented democratization of marketing in which a small player can effectively compete against very large companies. Big marketplace success is not a prerogative of only the large companies. Anyone with a great idea can effectively leverage social media and can get phenomenal visibility, have terrific impact, and build their brands in a very short period of time, giving these large companies a run for their money. All these developments have caught classical marketers unawares. The world moved fast past them, and many have really not been able to stay on top of their game in this changed paradigm. And all this was happening in the most recent Fourth Paradigm!

Typically, advertising and marketing expenses tend to be one of the significant expense items on the profit and loss statement, other than technology and people costs. In that scenario, many CEOs and CFOs could be looking at advertising and marketing dollars as a flexible and fungible resource they can pull from when in distress. When a marketer cannot clearly connect the dots between marketing activities and business outcomes, or they cannot quantify their business impact, they cannot defend their budgets. Typically, when asked what exactly marketing is doing for the bottom-line or top-line results and growth of the company, a marketer is like a deer caught in headlights. And when that happens, they are done for.

When their responses to financial questions are in terms of brand awareness, brand predisposition, net promoter scores, and a whole bunch of other important brand metrics, they have lost their audience and their credibility. Financial questions demand financial answers. Brand metrics are absolutely relevant and important, but typically, folks outside of marketing tend to care less about them. Also, brand metrics are perceived to have more mid- to long-term impact on business results, whereas promotions and offers have more immediate impact. So, the tendency of the CEO, CFO, or the business P&L owners is to push for sales generating campaigns, with the mind-set that we first need to deliver today to even be able to see a tomorrow. We will worry about tomorrow when tomorrow comes. Brand impact is over the long term, but in the long term, we are all dead anyway. So why worry about the brand?

Likewise, advertising and marketing awards are more relevant for the marketers. Candidly, those outside of marketing couldn't care two hoots about them. People have very little time, appreciation, or patience for those awards. Needless to say, they are, however, incredibly important for the marketing team and their agency partners—these are an acknowledgment and recognition of the great work they are doing, from their peers in the industry.

In my experience, I have seen marketers avoiding the tough questions from the CEOs and the CFOs. That doesn't serve them or their function well. That avoidance points to a lack of skill and command, and it erodes the credibility of the whole marketing function. People in sales, finance, and even many CEOs are quick to label the brand and the marketing function as soft and expendable. Unless marketers understand the foundational and finer aspects of the business, they are never going to be effective in positioning, defending, and advocating for the function.

Many CMOs and marketers tend to consider brand building, brand differentiation, brand positioning, and brand marketing as their most sacred responsibility. Then there is the other camp of companies, which focus on areas like performance marketing and operational marketing, with an emphasis primarily on driving numbers, getting sales leads, foot traffic, sales conversions, and so on. Performance marketers typically are in a much better position, as everyone in the company can see and comprehend a correlation between their actions and sales results. But their focus predominantly remains on day-to-day, week-to-week, or month-to-month performance. In many cases, these marketers, and therefore their companies, tend to neglect brand building. Because brand building is a long- to medium-term activity, the results are less conclusive. It's harder to establish the link between the brand strength and brand growth, or brand strength and business retention. And if marketers are purists focused solely on branding, they are perceived as fluffy, not understanding the business..

In the Fifth Paradigm, the mission of a Quantum Marketer has to be fourfold:

1. **Brand building.** In this day and age, the brand is not only sacred but vital for differentiation, value perception, and competitive advantage. Building a powerful brand is critical for the short-, medium-, and long-term health of the company. Marketers are brand stewards and need to build it for the future, irrespective of whether their business partners can fully appreciate it or not.

2. **Reputation management.** In many evolved companies, marketing and communications/PR have come together. After all, they are a single continuum. Marketing is the brand talking about itself. PR is getting other people to talk about the brand positively. When a social media post appears, it has the potential to create or destroy a brand; so, is that the responsibility of digital marketing or digital communications? It doesn't matter. The answer is yes! In a world where a ton of negative talk and fake news happens, many brands are going to get talked about in a poor light, sooner or later. Marketers absolutely need to have plans to defend their brands and protect their reputation and not let consumer trust erode. Whether it is brand building or managing a brand's reputation, it is brand management at the end of the day; and that is at the core of a Quantum Marketer.

3. **Driving business growth.** Marketing should be done not for the sake of marketing, but to help drive profitable business growth. This is a very important responsibility of marketing. Performance marketing helps drive overall business growth. In a company that is not really marketing driven, like the majority of organizations, unless the marketer takes on the responsibility for business growth and is really fueling the business, they will not be taken seriously. And to be fair, what is the point of building a magnificent brand if

it doesn't drive profitable business growth? Marketers should help drive business growth, whether or not it is in their formal mandate.

4. Creating platforms for sustained competitive advantage. The fourth pillar of Quantum Marketing is about building a sustainable competitive advantage via platforms, partnerships, Intellectual Property (IP), and so on. This is going to be a very significant and an important part of marketers' roles, particularly in contexts where they do not control all of the 4 Ps. They can still build a significant competitive advantage by building platforms that leverage marketing assets and marketing properties, and the IP that goes with it, to differentiate the brand and maintain the differential on a sustained, continuous basis for the long term. In other words, to build a strong, deep, and broad moat around the company and its products and solutions.

Many companies are not equipped well enough either by tech-savvy marketing talent or leadership, or competencies and capabilities, to tackle these four pillars (see Figure 3). That should be the first order of responsibility and focus for every CMO. Marketers come with many capabilities and strengths. There are classical marketers, contemporary marketers, performance marketers, and marketing innovators. A company needs a good and healthy mix of all four of these types of marketers. It needs to cross-fertilize and cross-train these people to be able to straddle multiple areas: quantitative marketing, qualitative marketing, performance marketing, the process management of marketing, or innovation within marketing.

THE FOURFOLD MISSION OF MARKETING

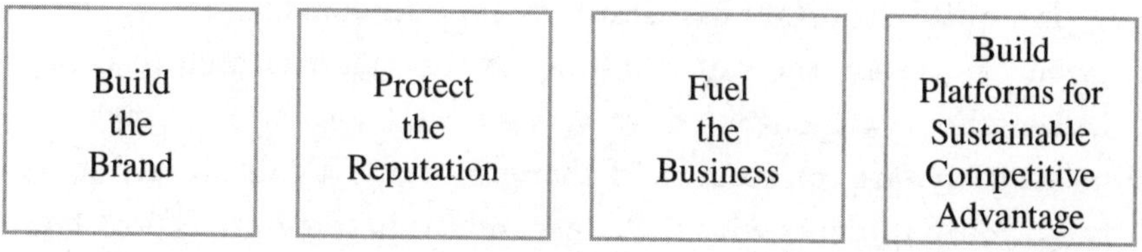

Build the Brand	Protect the Reputation	Fuel the Business	Build Platforms for Sustainable Competitive Advantage

FIGURE 3

Each one of these capabilities is going to set the company apart. With the advent of a whole slew of new technologies coming at us in the Fifth Paradigm, it is critical to have marketers who understand technology. A company also needs to have technologists, finance, procurement and legal specialists, data analysts, and risk managers embedded within marketing or supporting it from outside, pretty deeply. To be agile and effective, marketing needs to imbibe into its day-to-day activities depth across all these areas, as marketing will only get more complex. It is time that marketers really equip themselves to do justice both to their role and to the function.

The kind of talent to be attracted at the entry level will be crucial to the foundations of the marketing function into the future. However, amongst students coming out of college and looking to join companies, the top students are typically gravitating toward Silicon Valley or to entrepreneurship or to investment banks or consulting firms. Only a handful of people would say that marketing is their first choice. In fact, a 2019 study showed that engineering, nursing, and sales are the top three jobs for college grads. One would have to go to number six to find a marketing-related career (project management). A fascinating Association of National Advertisers (ANA) study recently showed just how far away marketing reality is from the university perception. Marketing, grads told the ANA, is "simply ads and selling." They found that a large number of students did not have an idea of what marketing does. Many of them even had negative impressions of marketing, as some sort of a con! It is a fascinating study, and horrific. It describes the awful state of the perceptions of marketing. ANA has even floated an initiative called "market marketing." It is indeed pretty apt and very much needed![1]

It is quite important to inspire and prep students for a marketing career. However, the case studies and the material used in many MBA schools are outdated. In this day and age, when things are moving forward so rapidly and changing daily, it's absolutely critical to equip students with the latest and the best materials possible. Many marketing professors practiced marketing before the advent of social media. They may benefit from a quick stint shadowing a few CMOs to observe the current day-to-day realities. Also, practicing marketers should provide to the universities the latest case studies to equip the professors to help build the next generation of marketing talent. CMOs and other senior marketers have to go to colleges, interact with the students, showcase the marketing function, and truly inspire them.

Sunil Gupta, marketing professor at Harvard Business School, agrees. "Marketing has dramatically changed in recent years," he told me. "It has become much more data driven and real time. The only way we can bring these new perspectives to our students is by constantly updating our own knowledge and by collaborating with industry leaders who are on the forefront of this revolution."

There simply is no other function as exciting and as poised to unlock the incredible opportunity and potential lying just ahead of us. It's going to be a fascinating time. There is no better time than now to be in marketing. And that's what we need to make the students understand. It's also important that people who grow in any organization should go through a stint in marketing before reaching the C-suite.

And the same is true for marketers. Before they reach the top levels in marketing, they should have to go through stints in some other functions and ideally get some profit-and-loss management experience under their belt. That is a recipe for success. I've been fortunate to have spent about half of my career managing P&Ls and the other half managing marketing as a function. My CEO, Ajay Banga, started his career in marketing and sales and grew through various business management roles to eventually assume the role of CEO of Mastercard. Banga became one of the most successful CEOs, stewarding the company over more than a decade through extraordinary growth and success. He understands the importance and value of marketing. Kudos to him; he has strongly advised that everyone in the company who is a general manager, before they reach the C-suite, has to have a stint within marketing. That is going to have a profound cultural impact in the company.

But it requires a CEO to drive it from the top of the house. And it is up to CMOs to earn the credibility and to demonstrate the value of marketing to their CEOs, particularly if those CEOs are not exposed to professional and hard-core marketing that has driven results.

Many companies in the packaged-goods industry have always led with marketing. The rest of the company rallies around the agenda set by marketing to make the company successful. But in other industries, marketing tends to be a support function. It is not a lead function. The agenda is set up by the business owner or by the sales head or the head of the country or region. The difference is important to recognize. When such a company hires somebody from a packaged-goods or FMCG (fast-moving consumer goods) industry, the new hire struggles with not being in charge. It's important in this day and age for marketers to understand that the hierarchy or who sets the agenda is not as important as what value and what contribution marketers can make to the company, what kind of influence they can have. If marketers adopt this kind of mind-set, the opportunities ahead of them are absolutely abundant. That is the winning mind-set for them to be a true business partner.

In order to truly reset the mission of marketing along the four pillars, today's marketer can no longer afford to be a marketing specialist. Quantum Marketers need to have a good understanding of data, digital technologies, communications and public relations, sales, business dynamics, company financials, growth drivers, and so on. They operate at the confluence of all these and many more functions. So, overall, a Quantum Marketer needs to be a versatile general manager with a deep knowledge of marketing, as opposed to someone who is a functional marketing specialist. They need to have a business manager's mind-set, with a deep understanding and a deep proclivity toward marketing. They need to be inspiring enough to get their teams to think big and outside the box, and guide them as needed.

Once, a CFO asked me, "What's the big deal about marketing?" In that person's mind, the marketer simply gives a brief to the agency, pays their fees, and approves the great ideas the agency comes up with—and that's about it. Unfortunately, when colleagues have zero understanding of what marketing is and can do, it is a tough uphill battle. But it's up to marketers to educate, convince, and tactfully influence their peers and colleagues. Nothing proves the value of the function better, in short order, to the company than showing improved business results via marketing efforts.

For a true reset, the CEO needs to endorse the mission of marketing. Some companies are more evolved and sophisticated, further along the journey and moving in the right direction. Others are further behind and need to come up the curve rather quickly because massive, massive quantum changes are just around the corner. And if not well prepared, the tsunami of competition and market forces will drown the marketing function and the company. But if prepared and positioned well, a company can unlock and unleash the true and enormous power of marketing.

It is time that we bring the glory and gravitas of marketing back. Let's start with a clear mission.

TO SUMMARIZE . . .

➤ Many companies are fragmenting and reducing the role of marketing in their organizations. This movement has its roots in an inability to keep pace with the dramatic advancements in technology and in data.

➤ The mission of a Quantum Marketer has to be fourfold:
  1. Brand building
  2. Reputation management
  3. Driving business growth
  4. Creating platforms for sustained competitive advantage

➤ CMOs need to earn the credibility and build a relationship with the CEO to transform the culture of the company to one that values and leverages marketing. And an empowered marketing function can unlock enormous potential for the company.

CHAPTER 4

The Data Dilemma

Once the marketer has the right mission, the next area of focus is on how to bring it to life and be able to execute on it. To be able to successfully thrive in the Fifth Paradigm, marketers need to gain a good grasp of and expertise in many areas. I will address them in this chapter and the chapters that follow, covering areas ranging from technology to the sciences behind marketing. But first things first. Marketers need to understand and gain command of data, data analytics, and AI. Data is the precious commodity in the Fifth Paradigm. Let's start exploring it.

I worked at Citibank from 1994 to 2009. Very early on, in 1995, I established the first data analytics unit in the UAE. The analysis was mostly used for the newly launched credit cards business then. And the results were immediately evident. From being one of the last entrants to the market, we quickly grew to be the market leader in that geography within just one year and established a robust, profitable business. Mind you, that market was predominantly cash driven and here we showed up with credit cards and drove both the category growth and our own brand growth. Since then, I have discovered the immense power data can bring to marketing. It has always been and always will be a powerful and indispensable tool in my marketing toolbox. In every industry I have been in since, I found data analytics to be one of the most significant drivers of sound strategy formulation and its efficient execution.

Given how much more vital data's role is going to be in the Fifth Paradigm, and given that most marketers come from the nonquantitative side of the house, I will cover in this chapter most aspects of data that a marketer needs to be aware of, in simple terms.

Data analytics in marketing came of age with credit card companies in the United States, which would send billions of direct mail pieces every year. For every million pieces they sent, hardly four thousand people would respond. That is just 0.40 percent. Put another way, 99.6 percent of their mail went straight to the trash bin. In some ways it was the ultimate example of "spray and pray" versus precise and efficient targeting.

So they began looking at new ways to identify prospects who were more likely to respond to direct mail on the one hand, but also, on the other, be most profitable to the company over the lifetime of the relationship. This required powerful data analytics, necessitating that acquisition marketers understand and leverage the power of data effectively. Those card companies and banks that knew how to leverage data had a substantial competitive advantage. Data was becoming the new currency to differentiate oneself and excel in the marketplace.

With the advent of enterprise-wide databases, marketers were able to compute lifetime values of their customers across all the relationships they had with the company. This enabled them to create relationship-based strategies, as opposed to product-based strategies.

With the arrival of Google and the various ad platforms, marketers who were leveraging the digital channels started genuinely appreciating the power of data, and they realized the opportunity to get to precise, targeted, and actionable insights as never before. It helped them refine their messages and create highly optimized promotions that would motivate consumers to choose their brand over the others. Marketers also had suddenly gained the ability to serve consumers with ads in a contextually relevant manner. They could measure return on marketing investment (ROMI), quite accurately. It became evident that it's not the raw data that provides competitive advantage, but the ability to play with, analyze, and act on data that provides competitive advantage.

All this required constant gathering of data, updating the database, cleaning the database, analyzing in as near real time as possible, and enabling both reactive and proactive actions. When marketers married their own data (first-party data) with third-party data bought from others, they significantly enriched the quality and depth of their insights further. That, in turn, made marketing significantly more effective.

Rohit Chauhan, executive vice president of artificial intelligence at Mastercard, summed it up very well: "Data is literally an ocean. You need a way to get your head around it and make sense out of it. If you boil everything down, you have three buckets of data: descriptive (what happened), predictive (what will happen), and prescriptive (what the dimensions of consumer data are). I can give a simple analogy that will demonstrate the difference among these. The companies that rely mostly on descriptive data are akin to driving their cars while looking in the rearview mirror. It is useful, but only up to a point. The companies which are using predictive data are forecasting the future and preparing for it. They are driving their car looking through the windshield and looking ahead at the road. Which is good. But what can be better than that? Driving with the help of a GPS! That is prescriptive data. It tells you where to take a right turn, how far you are from your destination, is there an accident or a pitfall ahead, etc. It takes your driving efficiency and effectiveness to a different level altogether."

That is indeed a brilliant way of capturing the gist! Prescriptive data is about not only looking back and looking forward but also looking at what is not visible to you at the moment.

DATA PRIVACY

Data is also a double-edged sword. As much as it gives insights to do relevant and effective marketing, it also can compromise consumers if the data is not well protected. For example, if a person goes to a hospital for some tests and that medical data falls into the wrong hands, that person can be in serious trouble. If the data falls into the hands of potential employers, they could use it to decide against hiring that individual because the health condition may raise red flags to the company in terms of the person's productivity and performance.

That kind of data availability and utilization can severely, adversely, and unfairly affect individuals and deprive them of opportunities. Hence, a slew of regulations was put in place to prevent people from abusing and misusing data. In the United States, HIPAA (Health Insurance Portability and Accountability Act) protects all health information and prevents potential misuse and abuse that can otherwise destroy people's lives. Ironically, and sadly, this kind of health-data protection is not in place in many countries, even today.

Different industries are at different levels of evolution on leveraging data. For example, the health-care industry, even in developed countries, is still in the dark ages as it pertains to data collection, data collation, and data sharing. Ideally, when a patient receives care in a hospital, physicians and clinical teams should have access to medical data from all of the patient's past medical encounters. This would give the care team a full picture of the patient's health condition. Unfortunately, hospitals' data standards and systems vary, making it difficult to accurately share patients' medical information that would ensure informed, high-quality care and optimal outcomes.

"The health-care industry has a tremendous opportunity to leverage data, enabling providers to learn more about a patient's history, particularly, those with chronic diseases," said John Starcher, president and CEO of Bon Secours Mercy Health. "The more we know about a patient's history and lifestyle, the more we can use innovative treatment approaches and predictive modeling to shape behaviors and keep patients healthy, rather than treating them when they're acutely ill. Data consolidation helps providers ensure they are providing the most appropriate, efficient, cost-effective healthcare services. Reducing unnecessary health-care costs is a priority for all health-care providers."

So, how is this relevant to marketers? Well, for marketers in the health-care industry, when health data is combined with lifestyle data (including what I buy, where I eat, etc.), the insights can be very powerful and help them design effective messaging strategies and create effective incentive and reward programs, custom designed to help the patient pursue and adhere to healthy habits and lifestyle.

SENSORS KNOW EVERY BREATH YOU TAKE

Now let's get into the Fifth Paradigm. If marketers thought they were already drowning in a tidal wave of data, just wait. Connected devices are everywhere, with many, many more to come. A mobile phone is a sensor on many levels. We use our mobile phones for everything from making calls to shopping, even tracking our health metrics. To a consumer, it is a virtual window to the world. And to the marketer, it is a virtual window into the consumer's life and lifestyle!

There are a slew of sensors already out there, and even more pouring in: smart bulbs (Philips), connected refrigerators (Samsung), smart dishwashers (Whirlpool), smart washing machines, and smarter driers (Maytag). And wearable devices: watches (Apple), rings (Oura), lockets (Evermée), clothes (Levi's), and shoes (Adidas) with sensors. Even connected sleep monitors (Owlet) and connected commodes (Kohler). Then there are smart thermostats (Nest), smart speakers (Alexa), and smart locks (Ring). Between all of them, they track every move you make, every breath you take . . . Reminds me of that song from The Police.

Every second, consumers are throwing out more data that can be gathered, collated, and analyzed.

The sheer quantum nature of data and the speed with which it is being spewed out is mind boggling. Companies need to rethink their entire data strategies and technology architecture for this imminent future. Which data is relevant and which is mere clutter? Companies need to guard against data greed, but they also need to make sure that they are not shortchanged by what they see as possibilities today versus how the world might evolve in unexpected directions tomorrow.

The availability of real-time data could be a real boon, but only if it is acted upon in real time. Marketers will probably stand to gain a lot competitively if they address consumers' contextual reality in real time, without being intrusive. So, the marketing technology, architecture, and processes need to be able to: capture data in real time; aggregate it and map it in a sensible and accurate manner; analyze it for specific or general insights; link those insights to potential actions; launch those actions through the most appropriate channels; measure the effectiveness, or lack thereof, of the campaign actions; update with further data received in the interim; analyze, rinse, and repeat. Real-time data assimilation and real-time analytics are both going to be absolutely essential, as also are real-time campaign development and execution capabilities, in the Fifth Paradigm.

A DAY IN THE DATA LIFE

Let me make it tangible, by describing how a day in the life of consumers might look . . .

They wake up in the morning. Their sleep monitor, wearable device, connected bed or smartphone, or all of the above know precisely when they woke up and will relay this information to the cloud. The devices know what quality of sleep they had. They go to the bathroom, brush their teeth with the connected toothbrush (courtesy P&G, which guides them to brush those hard to reach places they are not brushing well enough or to reduce the pressure in other areas where the teeth enamel is eroding), weigh themselves on the connected scale (courtesy Withings, which will alert them if they lost weight rather suddenly, signifying an impending congestive heart failure), use the commode fitted with urine and stool analyzing sensors and mechanisms (courtesy Phillips, which will be preprogrammed to do routine examinations and report if they find something nasty), use the connected shower (may be Koehler, which measures their water consumption and temperature, so it can suggest better ways to conserve water and not lower their blood pressure below a certain level due to excessive temperature), and take items from the connected refrigerator for their breakfast (courtesy Samsung, which will reorder items running low and can potentially keep a calorie count based on their consumption). Their connected toaster, microwave, and stove can cross-tabulate results with the data collected from the fridge to validate the amount and type of their consumption and overall eating habits and populate the data directly into their health app.

Then they get into their connected, autonomous car to get to someplace, and it will magically suggest where they can stop for a quick coffee, courtesy Starbucks, which knows they are on a particular route that happens to have one of its store locations there; in fact, the store is located there based on the previously collected traffic data from the autonomous cars and GPS trackers. When they go to get the coffee, their face is well known to the systems at Starbucks, so they don't have to worry about mundane things like payments—they all happen in the background. When they finally leave the car and step out, the nearest billboard on the way to their office building knows who they are, by triangulating a bunch of the data bread crumbs, and will let them know what special offers are there nearby, exclusively for them, just for that day (courtesy Qualcomm).

Yes, billboards will be able to serve ads that are customized just for that consumer. For a marketer, this medium is no different from a regular digital channel that can be accessed from a tablet or smartphone. It is just another new, versatile screen.

But all of this comes with a huge responsibility on the part of the marketers: to protect the privacy of the consumers. A 2019 Clearing House study shows consumers generally lack awareness of what data is being collected—for example, 80 percent are not fully aware that apps or third parties may store their bank account username and password. Consumers are also unaware of how long data can be accessed—for example, only 21 percent are aware that financial apps have access to their data until they revoke their bank account username and password.[1]

Apps are the main offenders. Another study, this one from a consortium of universities, showed that mobile devices from as many as two hundred vendors come preinstalled with software that collects user data. These apps can access the microphone, camera, and location without ever asking the end user. This potentially leaves consumers completely unaware of dangerous privacy intrusions.[2]

It will be a crazy world, if it's not already, of rushing to capture every bit of data about every aspect of the consumer from sunup to sundown, even during sleep. There is a Wild West–like rush to gather every data bread crumb, to be able to construct a picture of who the consumer is—supposedly, all with permission. But consumers often don't realize they are consenting to a slew of different devices and service providers to capture every data point vendors can lay their hands on. Typically, either as legal cover or from a quasi-unethical or exploitative tendency, companies serve digital reams of terms and conditions they ask consumers to accept before giving them access to their site or app or whatever. Honestly, who thinks that anyone reads them, other than the lawyers and geeks? Consumers, out of meekness or laziness or lack of choice, accept and sign their lives away. This is a brave new world. And it should not be this way. We will talk more about this in a later chapter on ethics.

Marketers need to be careful that sensors, or any other technology that follows a consumer's digital path, are transparent in their purpose. There have been some egregious examples of consumers unknowingly contributing personal data that companies have then sold. Consider what happens when someone sends a vial of saliva for DNA analysis, whether to learn their genealogy or to get personalized diet and medicine recommendations. The person knows they're sharing their DNA with a genomics company, even though they may have opted in to give permission, they may not realize that their data will be resold to pharmaceutical firms.[3]

Many apps use a consumer's location to serve up custom advertisements. Still, these apps don't make clear that some hedge fund may also buy that data to analyze behavior and inform their retail sales forecasts.[4] In most cases, such data sold is anonymized, which is a bit of a saving grace. But, still . . .

All this unbelievably humongous quantum of data is going into the cloud, with storage costs coming down by the second. And with the processing costs, too, coming down by the second, marketers can collate and organize this data, crunch it in real time, and come up with incredibly powerful and actionable insights.

A WORLD BEYOND COOKIES

Let's remember that privacy is a human right. Apple CEO Tim Cook said so very adamantly in 2018. He outlined four key privacy rights: the right to have personal data minimized; the right for users to know what data is collected on them; the right to access that data; and the right for that data to be kept securely.[5] And as the sensitivity to consumers' privacy protection gains momentum, we are already beginning to see some significant changes in the ad business. At the beginning of 2020, Google announced that it will prevent cookies from being installed on its browser over the next two to three years. Apple announced precisely that, a few months earlier.

This is excellent news for consumers. And it is a huge problem for marketers. (Welcome to the Fifth Paradigm!) Without cookies, how can marketers know consumer behavior and how can they target them effectively? And what about retargeting, which many categories of business, including retail, have used profitably? This move away from cookies will disrupt the ad business in a big way, without a doubt.

We can address a future without cookies, while also being consumer-friendly and protecting consumers' privacy. While there is no silver bullet, some organizations are trying to solve the problem. One such solution is digital ID. A consumer requests and is given a digital ID from verification consortia like Iden-Trust or GlobalSign. With consumers' permission and based on their preferences, that ID can be tagged with different elements of consumers' online and off-line behavior, enriching the ID profile or cleansing it. And the IDs themselves are highly encrypted and the data associated with any ID is encrypted at multiple levels of security. For example, a consumer's credit card or financial or health information will be much more strongly encrypted than the data about which news sites the person visits. This requires a whole new visualization of the ecosystem, the technology stack, the programs that manage these security protocols, the safe connectivity to service providers, and so on. And there will be a new genre of ID verification or authentication organizations. Could the digital ID live in a personal block on the blockchain? The answer is yes. In fact, more than fifty-seven companies in Asia have created a consortium called the MyID Alliance. Their goal is to put all identity credentials and financial information on individual blockchains.[6]

Similar solutions in different forms are emerging. For example, multiple companies can contribute their first-party data about consumers, obtained from consumers' visits to their own sites, to a single "clean" room. Consumers are then tagged with the data from these different sources, giving rich insights useful for future targeting. Various such approaches will be conceived in which the consumers' privacy is held paramount, cookies don't track consumers via any browsers, yet marketers and publishers in the data consortia get relevant insights to be able to do their business well.

Digital ID also presents a new spin on the data ownership issue. Could consumers own all access to their data and even sell it? Or at least get a share of the ad revenue in exchange for their data? We'll increasingly see this trend. Consumers will not only get access and information in exchange for their data and attention, as they do now, but they will also get paid over and above. Take a recent example: a new browser called Brave has already garnered ten million users in a relatively short time, with the promise that they would guard consumers' privacy and reward them for their data and attention.[7] The Brave browser combines ad blocking technology with a blockchain-based digital advertising platform. If consumers turn on the rewards option, they can earn frequent flier–like tokens for viewing privacy-respecting ads. Also, users can set the number of ads they want to see per hour. And this is just the beginning.

THE DARK SIDE OF DATA

Data is a potent currency. What happens if governments get hold of all the data about individuals? Is that the end of independence, freedom, and privacy? What happens when this data is obtained by people who can abuse it? How should marketers protect their consumers? How can a marketer act with purpose when data breaches happen, beyond giving them idiotic and unsatisfactory solutions like one year of credit bureau monitoring?

The dark side of data has found an all too comfortable home on the dark web. The dark web is not seen by standard browsers. A different browser, called Tor, is necessary to access it, and you can find a plethora of illegal goods and services there. It is a nefarious marketplace in which one can browse, sell, or buy things—from drugs to arms to tools and services that can be used to hack people's data and blackmail them. The bad actors hack emails, account numbers, identification credentials, and any other relevant information, and they put them up for sale on the dark web. The potential impact on individuals can be devastating. Credit lines and loans can be obtained fraudulently. Their names can be drawn into some nefarious acts that they will have hell trying to explain. Their emails and confidential information can be used to blackmail them. This is terrifying in every which way.

The crooks have been threatening not only consumers but enterprises too. At the end of 2019, Kerem Albayrak, a twenty-two-year-old man from North London, demanded that Apple give him either $75,000 in cryptocurrency or $100,000 in iTunes gift cards in exchange for him deleting what he claimed was a massive database of iCloud accounts. He was sentenced to two years for the threat.[8] But how many consumers or small companies have the resources and sophistication of an Apple?

Against this potential mayhem, marketers have to realize the consequences to consumers if the data they gathered is not well protected. Collecting data comes with the responsibility to guard it.

GDPR, CCPA, AND THE AFTERMATH

Some governments are trying to formulate data policies. The European Union has GDPR (Global Data Privacy Regulation), which is the first significant privacy legislation of its kind. Put simply, the GDPR leans on two concepts: consent and Privacy by Design. Privacy by Design is the name of an approach all businesses should now take when creating products and building websites. Privacy by Design involves keeping data collection to a minimum and building security measures into all stages of a product's design. Obtaining consent simply means asking users for permission to process their data. Companies must explain their data collection practices in clear and straightforward language, and then users must explicitly agree to them.[9]

In principle, GDPR is terrific, no question about it. As a consumer, I should have a right to know what data is being collected about me, a right to permit third parties to collect my information or not, a right to be forgotten, and a right that my data should be deleted from everywhere that I don't want it to be.

Following similar principles, the state of California has launched the California Consumer Privacy Act (CCPA), which went into effect at the beginning of 2020. And there is momentum to adopt similar laws around the world. It will be an area that will be regulated and enforced.

Working closely with policy makers, companies must set parameters for protecting people's data rights and, equally, make sure the policies are pragmatic, so companies will comply. We need ways to detect the bad actors, as they can otherwise vitiate the whole ecosystem. And there needs to be consequences for violating privacy standards, whether the violators are domestic or beyond our borders. We also need to make sure governments do not abuse data themselves. We are all aware of the case in which the US government tried to force Apple to give a backdoor entry into their phones. The government had no harmful intent but wanted to get to potential terrorists and prevent acts of terrorism. A noble intention. But those kinds of backdoor openings, as Tim Cook correctly says, open the doors for all the hackers, too, which would devastate the security of their ecosystem for everyone. Now, where do you draw the line? This is one really complex world, with no easy solutions.

DATA DEMOCRATIZATION AND OPEN MARKETING

Another interesting policy area that is fraught with both pros and cons is a facet of data democratization. Consider the following very powerful scenario: in the European Union, the policy makers determined that banks should open up their consumer data, with consumers' permission, to fintech and other companies, as a way to level the playing field and to also drive innovation. The primary premise there was the data pertaining to the consumers' transactions belonged to consumers and they could ask the banks for their information to be shared. That gave birth to the whole concept of Open Banking, which is transforming the banking and fintech space. Ashok Vaswani, CEO of Retail Banking and Payments of Barclays, aptly says, "The landscape is transforming in such a big way that the rules of the game have changed. Everyone needs to rethink their go-to-market strategies. In the past, we always asked the customers to come to us—our branch, our phone, our website, or our app. Now, for the first time, we can go to the customers exactly wherever they are. The old ways are giving way to high-precision, laser-guided tactics. Businesses and marketers have to rethink everything from strategy to talent to capabilities and skill sets."

In much the same way, could that concept of Open Banking be extended to marketing, i.e., Open Marketing? It means that companies like Amazon, Google, Facebook, or others may need to share the data they hold about consumers' transactions, posts, searches, etc., with other companies, so the field currently dominated by a few digital giants can be more leveled for others to compete effectively. Whether it happens in a big way or in specific portions of the ecosystem, it is definitely going to happen. This is really an exciting new dimension that will define Quantum Marketing.

TO SUMMARIZE . . .

➤ **Take the lead.** No other group of professionals has the volume of data collection on consumers, day to day, as marketers do. And a significant part of the data ecosystem is funded out of marketing dollars. Marketers, therefore, have to play a front and center role and drive the evolution, as opposed to sitting in a corner and letting others define the future.

➤ **Educate yourself.** Marketers need to understand the current policies and regulations across the entire value chain they deal with. They need to understand how data is collected, organized, and analyzed in real time, with or without the help of AI. Marketers don't need to become data experts overnight, but they need to educate themselves at least to the extent of being able to ask the right questions and grasp the right answers.

➤ **Invest in the right partnerships—internal and external.** Strike deep partnerships with IT colleagues who manage the data infrastructure and processes, as well as legal department colleagues to help navigate this complex ecosystem soundly and safely. Marketers' accountability doesn't end with protecting consumer data within their company; it also extends to the data that their vendors are collecting, analyzing, and leveraging on their behalf. Marketers need to understand whether they have the wherewithal to protect consumers' data against any attacks or any breaches and compromises. Ditto with their agencies who handle data on their behalf.

➤ **Beware of the BS out there.** Hemingway said that the most important thing for a writer was a built-in bull**it detector. Same for data. Every vendor and his cousin come to the table saying that their solution is powered by AI. Ask the vendors to simplify what they're talking about. Sort out the signal from the noise. Marketers need to have experts on their side, if they themselves are not experts.

➤ **Don't be carried away by jargon.** Predictive coding, transformative synergy, untapped vertical, deep neural networks... C'mon. Marketers need to have folks on their teams who understand data and who can also speak plain English, not jar-gonese. The team members will be thankful!

➤ **Have deep data talent within marketing itself.** There's no rule that says marketing can't have data scientists. No rule that says marketing can't have AI subject matter experts or team members with technology experience. Get the team members trained in data very deeply.

➤ **Use Privacy by Design standards.** This phrase showed up as the GDPR advanced. It means companies are obliged to con-sider data privacy during design stages of all projects along with the life cycle of the relevant data process.[10] Follow that approach and implement that principle. Marketers, you'll thank yourselves for this later!

➤ **Secure the data.** This is a huge issue with so many hacks being attempted on all databases every second from around the world. Cybersecurity broadly, and information security in particular, should be a top priority for every organization and for every marketer.

➤ **Stay close to industry developments.** I set aside at least six hours a week for keeping up on learning and keeping up with industry news. Bottom line, change has implications. Don't get caught unaware. Stay very current. The time is well spent and the effort well worth it.

➤ **Quantify, quantify, quantify.** Even if you have a futuristic AI program, if you don't diligently measure marketing actions, your company will not understand their contribution to sales, overall revenue, or the overall business. Defending marketing by qualitative arguments or worse, marketing jargon, will prove rather futile. Be ready with credible numbers, not words.

➤ **Don't let data overshadow creativity.** Don't forget that it is about the brand, the business, and the competitive platform. Technology and data are absolute priorities, but not at the cost of creativity, instinct, and judgment.

Above all, two things. First, ask the tough questions. Marketers need to ask themselves how they would want others to use their data. Then they should put on their marketing hats and follow those principles while respecting the regulations. If something about their data leverage doesn't feel right, it means it is not.

Second, play offense. Data gives us the power to do the right thing by the consumer, to serve them most effectively, in the most relevant way. And, most pleasantly, marketers can serve those offers that matter to their consumers. Marketers should not be staying on the data sidelines.

CHAPTER 5

AI

The Ultimate Propellant of Quantum Marketing

Mario Klingemann describes himself as a skeptic. At least on the Sotheby's fine art website he does. As someone who commands $40,000 per work of art, it's hard to believe him. His works have been compared to the Dutch Masters, and he has been praised for the "aesthetic principles in his work." Skeptic is as skeptic does. Klingemann is not a painter, and his success in the art world comes not from brushes but from algorithms. Klingemann is truly a master. A master of artificial intelligence.[1]

And his story happens with frequency. There's Scott Eaton, who sculpts incredibly lifelike human limbs using AI algorithms.[2] Or Refik Anadol, who creates amazing pieces of art and architecture based on vast data sets (like the temperature in different parts of the world) using machine intelligence.[3]

A lot is being spoken and written about AI and how it changes everything in our world. Some of it is pure gimmickry, some of it is sheer noise, and some of it is real and truly astounding.

But before we unpack AI, let's review the central concept of this book. Quantum, for our purposes, means two things. First, it means that past models will be unable to explain future reality. Second, the speed, scale, and impact of Quantum Marketing are unprecedented. Nothing fits this concept in the new paradigm quite like artificial intelligence does.

AI will be a completely disrupting force in the Fifth Paradigm. But first, it's useful to quickly go back through the five paradigms from a data perspective. Data, as we know it today, was not really a huge driver within marketing in the first two paradigms. In the Third Paradigm, the internet exploded, and consumer behavioral data became abundant and widely available. The analysis of data, hitherto deployed in more nerdy fields, arrived in marketing. And the new science of data analytics started helping marketers in many ways, from precision targeting to ROI computations and everything in between. It took marketing to a new scientific level.

In the Fourth Paradigm, with mobile devices becoming ubiquitous and connected, and with the advent of social media platforms, the entire marketing model was stood on its head, and the marketing approach had to be significantly reimagined. Areas like social marketing, influencer marketing, location-based marketing, and so on took off. Marketing was never going to be the same again. In this Fourth Paradigm, data was being generated at extraordinary levels. The capabilities around data and data analytics became highly democratized. This meant that even small companies could effectively leverage the power of data, execute targeting across the split screens, measure effectiveness, and refine their approach. They could compete and give hell to the large, established companies, which earlier were the only ones with the scale and the deep pockets to do all this. Neither were necessary going forward. What could be better for a marketing executive?

Enter AI. It is the perfect Fifth Paradigm example because it takes a simple concept (consumer data) and brings it to a territory that could never be predicted or foreseen. AI in the Fifth Paradigm will be the Large Hadron Collider of data, producing controlled explosions with radical results.

I heard a few marketers say, "Why do I need to know AI? I don't need to know how electricity is generated or how electricity works, so long as I know that if I turn the light switch on, the bulb lights up."

Well, any good marketer should better learn. They are more than just a layperson switching on a light. AI is going to be a game changer in every aspect of marketing. If they don't understand the way it works and the possibilities it can bring, they will be missing the boat. AI will never replace marketers. But marketers who resist it will be replaced by those who understand its power. At this stage of the evolution of AI in the context of marketing, it is important for marketers to get their head around it. Iconic designer Charles Eames said it brilliantly: "Never delegate understanding."

There are a lot of companies coming out of the woodwork saying their solution is powered by AI. Marketers need to know what to believe and what to discount. They need at least a certain level of basic knowledge to understand what is being said, discern if it is truthful or valuable, and make a call as to whether to deploy it. Equally, marketers need to have their teams learn and stay up to date.

WHAT IS AI?

Artificial intelligence is a machine capability created by training machines to be able to think like human beings or even surpass them. That includes various forms of recognition, reasoning, judgment, decision-making, and so on. There are three types of artificial intelligence: Artificial Narrow Intelligence, Artificial General Intelligence, and Artificial Super Intelligence.

Artificial Narrow Intelligence is the ability of the machine confined to one single area or field, for example, to recognize images. All that machine will be able to do is just that one thing and nothing else. While it recognizes images, it will not be able to recognize voices, for example.

Artificial General Intelligence, on the other hand, will be more versatile and have broader capabilities. Just like a human being, it will be able to think and perform in multiple areas—recognizing voices and images, making judgments, writing poetry, and yes, creating ads.

Artificial Super Intelligence, as the name suggests, is where the machine will have human-like thinking capabilities but is far superior to human thinking. The machine can outlearn, outthink, and outperform human beings in every area. More so, it does all this quite independently, without any human intervention.

Various leading minds in this field agree that Artificial General Intelligence and Artificial Super Intelligence are still distant aspirations and may not materialize for decades. On the other hand, Artificial Narrow Intelligence, which is what people mean when they generally say AI, is here and now and is gaining momentum day by day, at an extraordinary pace. This is what we will focus on in this chapter.

Let's also look at two other terms that are constantly bandied around these days, and let me demystify them.

➤ **Machine learning.** In traditional computer programming, the computer is given clear and step-by-step instructions on what to do first, then next and next and so on. Every step is coded for the machine to simply follow. On the other hand, machine learning is when the machine or computer (that is, the algorithms of the machine) is trained to perform tasks by learning by itself from previous data and examples. For example, let's say we are training the machine to recognize dogs. It is shown a picture of a dog and it tags it as a dog. Then another and another and another. We also show it pictures that have no dogs. When it tags a picture of a tree as a dog, we let it know that it is not. It will then learn that the image is not that of a dog. Over a period of time, it gets exposed to zillions of pictures of dogs, and it is able to accurately say which is a dog and which is not. To me, this is almost the same as how we teach babies to recognize a dog. We can teach the machine to recognize any image and identify what it is. It can also advance, and indeed has, to an extent that it can say who is who and who is not who they say they are. Facial recognition is one clear application of all this. But because this is a machine trained for image recognition only, that is all it will do, and a different machine will be needed to do a different kind of task.

➤ **Deep learning.** I look at deep learning as machine learning on steroids. In deep learning, the machine has layers of what are called neural networks, through which data is fed and processed differently than in machine learning. Deep learning can be extremely helpful in areas like speech recognition, pattern recognition, image recognition, and so on, and it has an extremely high level of accuracy and speed.

Now, what is beautiful about AI is how it handles a typical problem. For example, two plus two is four. That's the right answer. Existing algorithms do that easily. But artificial intelligence looks at the inputs and the answers and figures out the equation. In a typical algorithm of today, a computer is given the inputs and the mathematical equation, and it churns out the output rapidly. In AI, the inputs and the output are given and the computer figures out the mathematical equation. So, once it figures out that equation, when new data is presented, it predicts the outcome extremely well. This brings a completely new and powerful path to insights.

In a marketing parlance, AI can bring richness to every step of the marketing life cycle. It brings a deeper level of understanding not hitherto possible. For example, before AI, we would do correlation analysis or causal analysis, trying to find out which promotion or what level of discount or some other feature works best to drive the most conversions. In classical marketing, these were done via surveys, test marketing, factor analysis, past campaign response metrics, past promotion metrics, and so on. We would then come up with actionable insights or the right type and level of promotions. In more recent times, we added A-B testing and rapid analysis to determine what works and what doesn't.

But these were typically done at a segment level (a group of consumers with common characteristics) or at an aggregated level. For example, a company offers varying discounts to test which works best—say, 10 percent, 20 percent, and 30 percent. The sales lift for each discount can be measured in the aggregate, and a simple cost-benefit analysis can be done: How much does the company give up in exchange for getting a higher conversion? If it gets an 8 percent lift in conversions at a 20 percent discount and a 10 percent lift at 30 percent, it may conclude that a 20 percent discount is economically better. This way, in an iterative fashion, the company can determine an optimal discount level.

But bear in mind, this optimal point is for a given segment, not for each individual in that segment. For example, I may be in the segment that the marketer determined responded optimally at a 20 percent discount. But I would have responded positively to a 10 percent discount, so the company wasted the extra discount on me. Using AI, on the other hand, the company can analyze my past behavior, my current propensity to buy in the category, and my behavior in other categories. This may give a clue into my overall attitude toward discounts and levels of discounts. This analysis is done in real time, and the company will be able to send me a highly personalized offer that is good for me and great for the company.

With AI, it is possible to ferret out patterns and relationships across a vast number of databases, across incredible amounts of data, which is not really possible with traditional data analytics.

As we enter the Fifth Paradigm, data will be produced and gathered at a rate that is both unprecedented and unpredictable. One of the key drivers for this will be sensors, which gather and spew out data continuously and add a new dimension over and above all that is generated today. Sensors will be a significant enabler of Quantum Marketing.

In the Fifth Paradigm everything will have a sensor, from watches to shoes, to cars, golf clubs, thermostats . . . everything. Every single second, the sensors are capturing data. All that data will be fed into AI machines. And it can throw out amazing patterns and insights from that macrocosm of data. This can help marketers if they can hook into that stream of insights and act on them in real time, to catch consumers at the most optimal parts of their daily life journey and offer them highly personalized products, services, promotions, and messages in a highly relevant fashion. The company can go from one OTM (opportunity to market) to the next OTM in a seamless, nonintrusive, nonannoying fashion.

AI will impact every part of marketing. We have just looked at a couple of areas. One is insights. And the other one is about running a campaign in a highly personalized, relevant fashion. Now, let's take a look at some of the other areas.

Chatbots

Chatbots powered by AI are becoming more and more human like, by the day. The result is that brands can serve their consumers very compellingly. The economics will be equally compelling too. For example, by deploying AI, companies will be able to save up to $8 billion per year in 2022,[4] because they can cut down on personnel and related expenses. In Quantum Marketing, AI deployment via chatbots will be the norm.

Virtual Assistants

While chatbots look only into the company database and respond, virtual assistants are much broader—they look at external data, too, such as from the internet. There is a higher order AI deployment in these virtual assistants. Alexa from Amazon, Google Home, and Siri from Apple are all some very well-known virtual assistants. What we will see in the Quantum Marketing world is that virtual assistants will become ubiquitous, even among brands that don't have hardware or devices. Today, many companies across various industries already deploy these virtual assistants to complement, if not replace, their existing human-powered concierge services. In the Fifth Paradigm, virtual assistants will proliferate, their quality will take a huge leap, and they will become an integral part of marketing channels. Additionally, virtual assistants will enter in a big way into new domains like health care, education, government, and so on.

Search

Google and its peers deploy AI in their search engines. As their AI gets smarter by the day, the search results get even more highly relevant and totally appropriate to the consumer. For most brands, showing up in search results is key to survival. Marketers need to adapt their own SEO algorithms as the search process keeps getting more intelligent.

Targeting and Personalization

Because AI can figure out the algorithms for prediction, it can help target precisely the people a company would want to win. Not only that, it will also help construct the kind of offer or message that would be most appropriate to a given prospect.

Media Buying

AI is already in the media buying space. With more and more media options coming about, with the advent of wearables and the Internet of Things, smart speakers, and so on, the complexity of media buying will increase exponentially. AI will play the central role, if not become the only player, in running the ecosystem. Already a number of media agencies see an erosion of their traditional roles. This will accelerate, and a new set of roles will emerge. New processes and dynamics will ensue.

Content Creation

Today already, an excess of content exists, and a lot of it is fake. For example, a video of President Obama saying things that of course he never did. But the video looks stunningly real. Likewise, there are photos of people who don't exist but were created pixel by pixel who look incredibly real. Check out the site ThisPersonDoesNot Exist.com. AI will exacerbate these fakes in a big way, because it's so easy to leverage the technology to create what are called deepfakes. There are any number of examples out there on the net, to showcase deepfake capabilities. With an explosion of real and fake content, with increasingly shorter shelf lives, marketers need to be incredibly thoughtful of the content they will create, how they authenticate it as real, and how to cut through—rather than adding to—the clutter. Studying people's online viewing behavior, we find that content needs to be created in real time to be not only appropriate but compelling to consumers. This creation of content will be done with the help of AI.

Ads are also content. Will ads be created by AI? There are staunch believers on either side of the aisle. While Artificial General Intelligence will make this happen, it is decades away. But even with current AI capabilities, static banner ads are already being autonomously created. I believe, over the next few years, a lot of creative compilation will happen—not original creativity though. The compilation might be so compelling that it could give the impression of being original.

In 2016, I witnessed an AI demonstration at Cannes Lions, an international festival of creativity. The AI engine was shown all the works of Rembrandt. It learned exactly how Rembrandt painted such as the direction of the brushstrokes, the length of the brushstrokes, the angles of the brushstrokes, and so on. Once it was trained, with 168,263 painting fragments, it was given a subject to paint. Voilà, a new Rembrandt painting, with 148 million pixels, was born! And a lot of experts have concluded that it is so closely authentic to Rembrandt that it is amazing. The demonstration won two Grand Prix for Cyber and Creative Data for JWT Amsterdam.[5] In just two years since, that kind of capability has come to apps, where a photo of anything can be uploaded and the app will immediately convert it into different styles of various classical or contemporary painters. That's how rapidly AI is becoming accessible.

AI is also writing articles in very authentic styles of various journalists and writers. It studies the works of an author, and when given a topic, it researches on the internet for relevant content and writes, in a matter of a few seconds, an article that mostly makes sense, in a style that seems authentic.

AI has begun composing (compiling is more like it) music. We have also seen the first contract between an AI engine and a record label! Warner Music Group signed the contract in 2019 with an AI algorithm created by start-up company Endel. And the contract is for twenty albums![6]

ROI Computation

ROI computation and accurate attribution to marketing activity have always been a challenge for most marketers. Some AI-based solutions can already estimate ROI in advance of a campaign or promo. If AI is appropriately incorporated into the marketing stream of consciousness, it will be able to come up with better ROI computation methodologies to predict, as well as to measure after the fact, what the ROI is.

LAUNCHING AI INITIATIVES

A company doesn't have to be large to deploy or leverage AI. The field, like data analytics before it, has been highly democratized. A company can start small and use open-source AI solutions such as Google TensorFlow or Amazon SageMaker. Marketers can also leverage off-the-shelf AI solutions, like Google's Vision API or Google's Speech API. Companies don't need to create those fundamental foundational functionalities. Marketers also don't have to invest large amounts—as they can avail themselves of "pay as you go" options. The only limit is their intent and imagination.

TO SUMMARIZE . . .

➤ Nothing is going to change the field of marketing more than AI. From learning about consumers deeply to enabling hyper-personalization to optimizing programs on the fly, AI can hugely enhance marketing effectiveness and efficiency.

➤ If marketers want to protect themselves from becoming obsolete, they have to familiarize themselves with AI. Better still, they need to learn it and learn it well.

➤ Marketers need to get their toes into AI right now. They can begin with low-cost pilots with a small project.

➤ Marketers can use off-the-shelf solutions. And there are many from big companies like Amazon and Google as well as a slew of start-ups.

➤ CMOs should get their teams educated on AI, an essential skill for the future. CMOs might even consider reevaluating roles on their team to ensure that that they are organized with the right people in place and on the case.

➤ Marketers don't need to become AI experts themselves, but they do need to know how to leverage AI. There are several online executive education programs from Harvard, MIT, and the University of California at Berkeley, to name a few.

➤ The IT department in a company has a significant role to play in this AI journey. Marketers absolutely need to partner with their IT colleagues to be collectively successful.

CHAPTER 6

Technology's Big Bang

A s AI fuels the explosion of data insights for marketers, get ready for a series of new technologies that will add new challenges and new opportunities. We are at that juncture in our evolution as a society where there is an astonishing level of technology development and deployment building off the Fourth Paradigm.

Before going boldly into the future, let's tip our hat to the three significant developments that transformed our world in the Fourth Paradigm.

1. We had the radical expansion of memory and processing capacities, with a dramatic reduction in costs. This enabled us to put enormous computing power into devices.

2. We have also seen a quantum leap in the design of the user experience, which made it very simple for even very young babies or older people to use these new devices without much, if any, training. For example, YouTube videos show small babies not ready to talk or walk happily using a tablet, very nicely. And as Moore's law hypothesized, the processing power and memory are doubling every two years, even as costs are coming down by half in that period. This law has held very well till now. The result? You have smart mobile devices with more computing power than Apollo 11 connected to the internet everywhere while fitting into the hands and budgets of most consumers around the world.

3. As a result of this access, social media platforms took the world by storm, bringing interpersonal digital interactions to a different level. Classmates discovered and connected after decades. Parents and grandparents could connect with and see their children and grandchildren live, and people were pouring out their hearts and minds via pictures, words, and emojis, openly and somewhat scarily so. People were discussing brands without the brands being in the conversation, and brand images were being built or destroyed by single social media posts.

As a result of all of the above, marketing had to find out new ways of cutting through the clutter, connecting with consumers, engaging them, and influencing their brand preference. Marketing was transformed completely, so much so that today more than 40 to 50 percent of all media dollars are put behind channels that did not even exist around the beginning of this millennium.

Now, as I alluded to in chapter 2, what is going to happen in the Fifth Paradigm is far more dramatic and explosive. A slew of compelling technologies are coming at us in a torrent, as you can see in Figure 4.

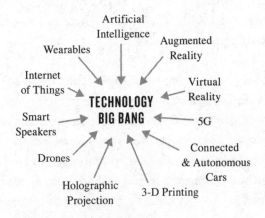

FIGURE 4

Beyond artificial intelligence, machine learning, and deep learning, which we spoke about in the last chapter, here is what we have in store:

5G

What's the big deal about fifth-generation cellular wireless? Everything.

➤ It is superfast, maybe fifty to a hundred times faster than 4G, with download speeds that could be as high as a hundred gigabits per second. In plain speak, this means that an entire movie on a standard DVD can be downloaded in less than four seconds.

➤ 5G can connect with more devices at once. That capability is what would power the Internet of Things, a wide variety of sensors, connected cars, autonomous vehicles, and so on and still not slow things down.

➤ 5G has very low latency. This means that there is no delay between a command at one end of the network and when it is executed on the other end. A surgeon moves her fingers in Los Angeles, and robotic fingers in the Miami operating room follow along precisely in almost the same instant. In a 5G environment, doctors can perform remote surgeries with confidence.

What are the implications for marketers?

The high speed with which data will be gathered and moved over various networks, combined with the low latency and AI, will make it possible to do real-time analytics, give consumers real-time solutions, create a high level of personalization, and be contextually appropriate and relevant. To put it simply, interactions and engagement strategies with consumers will be in real time. Let's look at an example. A consumer is shopping in a market. Based on her data, picked up with her permission, a company can make offers that are most relevant to where she is right now and what she is doing at this moment.

This is available now, but with 5G and AI, marketers can model her behavior right up to the second. Let's say the consumer is in a mall. Thanks to her mobile phone, her location is transmitted to the servers continuously, so her real-time location is known. If she makes a purchase, today, the purchase details don't get uploaded into the databases in real time. So, only locational details are available to the marketer, not the purchase details. But in the Fifth Paradigm, purchase details will also be available. Even so, we need rapid analysis and modeling to determine and execute the best offer or message for her. That requires not just computing power but data transmission at super speeds in a large bandwidth. This may feel like Big Brother on the face of it, but all this can and will be done in a totally anonymized way, protecting the consumer's privacy and bound by the data permissions she has put in place.

Another interesting area of application of 5G is in web design. Because of the speed and the bandwidth available in 5G, marketers need to rethink their web design. Currently, they don't want too many "heavy" pages with videos and visuals—they want a lean design to enable faster downloads. But going forward, that is not going to be an issue. Putting the current framework on its head, marketers would actually want to have rich and heavy pages.

Yet another interesting application is how customer service will be delivered remotely via call centers. Because the speed is so high, consumers can have live interactions via mobile video without any buffering or disruptions. So, companies would leverage that to have live video interactions with their consumers. That means that marketers need to rethink the customer experience design and rethink their customer service framework. Mobile VR and AR are going to throw open a tremendous opportunity in the customer service, sales, and engagement space.

Overall, 5G is a significant technological leap that will enable and transform other technologies and platforms in an unprecedented fashion. And marketing will benefit greatly. Marketers need to look at not just classical or traditional areas of marketing that will be impacted by 5G, but also at the intersections with other areas or functions that can be amped up by Quantum Marketing to drive business, brand, and competitive advantage.

AUGMENTED REALITY (AR)

AR is still very nascent, but it is going to become very big, very soon. In augmented reality, there is an overlay of digital information on a physical environment. For example, Google demonstrated at a conference how Google Maps will go to a different level by deploying what they call the Visual Positioning System, or VPS. When the smartphone's camera is pointed at the street, the Google Maps application will overlay the street scene with the map and an extra layer of information, such as a label or a flag indicating a coffee shop in one of the buildings up ahead. So, without having to walk down the street to see what shop it is, Google Maps will show you.[1] This is absolutely brilliant and makes consumers' lives so much easier.

Along with the names of shops, just about any other piece of information can be overlaid in the visual frame. Example: there is a sale going on in this shop; there is a special offer in this other shop; this is happy hour at this bar . . . You get the sense.

There is a new richness in terms of consumers' ability to interact with their physical environment. The opportunities are amazing for this, and very disruptive. Say I am traveling on vacation to a town in a different country. Armed with my AR app, I don't need a tour guide anymore. I can find my way and search for and see where the interesting spots are or where special offers are going on, right there in the app, which will also show me the shortest route to get there. What I see in front of my eyes is what I will see on my screen, except that the picture on the screen is now enriched with the extra, relevant, useful, and rich information that gets overlaid. Just imagine the marketing possibilities for a functionality like this.

Let's look at another example. When consumers receive their credit card by mail, they normally get a welcome package along with it. The welcome package has got a brochure that explains all the features, benefits, and offers on the card. They would probably take a look at the welcome brochure for a minute or less and throw it into the garbage bin. These brochures are a very static mode of communicating. How can we make sure that consumers, at any point in time, can find out the latest and the greatest about their card? All they need to do is open the AR app and focus it on the card. The app identifies the card and immediately displays against the card backdrop the various offers and benefits, like special access, available to cardmembers.

This is a very powerful and dynamic way of communicating benefits. The card issuers can stop incurring welcome brochure expenses and, at the same time, always keep their key member benefits updated into the app. They can also serve only the most contextually relevant and appropriate offers and benefits. Consumers don't get bombarded with offers available around the world but only those specific to their neighborhood, current location, or imminent destination. In essence, AR makes communicating offers highly engaging, and very simple, without the data overload and clutter. This same concept could be extended to appliances: the consumer could open the AR app, point the phone, and up will come the user manuals. Or when pointed at a food package, it can bring up nutritional information, or bring up recipes if pointed toward raw vegetables.

Let's look at yet another exciting example. A consumer walking by a clothing store sees a shirt that catches her eye in a window display. She simply takes out her AR app and points it at the item. The app brings up all the information about that shirt—the price, the manufacturer, where it is produced, the material it is made of colors and sizes available in the store at that point in time, what can be ordered online, what discount or promotion may be on offer, and so on. It completely changes what a shop window is: it's now a virtual or second shop for the store owner.

Companies like IKEA have already started leveraging the power of AR in yet another area. With its app, a consumer can view, quite realistically, different IKEA items virutally placed into their living room and get a good idea of how they will fit and look in that room.[2] It is a fantastic visualization tool. It takes imagination and guesswork out of the process. Likewise, AR is being deployed in a post-COVID-19 world, where consumers prefer touch-free experiences and are hesitant to try out cosmetics in a shop to see if they like the color of the lipstick or whatever. They can pull their AR app, point it at the lipstick, and the app shows how the color and texture would look on them, so they can decide if they like it. Ditto with trying clothes, where the mirror can bring out the AR layer to show the consumers how they look in a particular outfit. They can even try out different colors in a given outfit, without changing what they are wearing. It is the AR layer that does the trick. Experimentation has been going on for a while in this space, but what we will see in the Fifth Paradigm is the proliferation of use cases on the one hand and the wide prevalence on the other.

But, for marketers, there are still issues to be thought through. When people are walking on the streets, with their AR app, they will be seeing a ton of information popping up on their screens, layered over the physical space in front of them. How can a brand get into that stream of consciousness and show up smartly? If there are hundreds of brands that have hundreds of promotions and each one is cluttering up the screen space, it's not going to be effective. But the brands still need to stand out. How do marketers make sure that their brands stand out, attract the consumers' attention, and engage them effectively? This is going to be a fascinating way to rethink the entire model, the whole framework of how a brand would approach consumer attention, engagement, and commerce.

VIRTUAL REALITY

Virtual reality started with big hype but has been slow in coming. This is the technology that gives an immersive 360-degree view of everything. Users feel transported into the midst of whatever it is that they are viewing. This is a technology with a huge potential, but it has some ways to go in terms of quality, as the visuals are still fairly pixelated. Users get a bit of motion sickness if they are watching something moving, and they've got to wear a headset on their faces, which in itself is not a great experience.

But this just the beginning. Treat it as a proof of concept that's demonstrating to marketers the possibilities of this technology. VR is going to evolve on many fronts, beyond just the quality of the visuals. The units themselves will become sleek and comfortable. The cost of producing top quality VR videos, end to end, will come down dramatically. AR layers will be overlaid within the VR environment. Advances will be there to further enhance the immersive experiences, with elements like sound that would adjust based on which element a consumer is watching. Payments will be seamlessly integrated to make instant purchases.

Examples: A manufacturer of expensive chandeliers produces two museum-quality pieces, which are very expensive to stock, fragile to transport, and take up a lot of store display space. The company has several stores in various locations around the world. So, they need to figure out where these chandeliers are most likely to sell and display them there alone, missing out on the opportunity to display them at the other stores. They can always put videos and posters in other shops, but it is not likely anyone will buy these expensive items from videos and posters.

Enter VR. The company will produce a highly immersive and interactive video of the chandelier from all angles to bring out its grandeur, look, feel, and texture. That VR video gives the consumer a highly realistic, lifelike immersive experience of the chandelier. This can nudge the consumer toward the purchase. Every store can carry that VR video and give the prospects a realistic virtual experience. Overlaid with a layer of AR, the interactivity can be brought to life in an astounding way.

What happened here is that this chandelier company has just overcome a vast distribution and merchandising challenge. Marketers can think of all kinds of applications, across industries and product categories. For example, airlines can showcase their first-class cabins or hotels can showcase their rooms and suites, complete with great views. In some sense, these service providers are doing virtual sampling. Marriott has already started using this for some of its properties.[3] VR can have a profound impact on a company's merchandising, sampling, and consumer-engagement strategies.

Viewing live events like concerts and sports is going to be a huge VR application. Think about this: Do marketers want to show 2-D ads to viewers watching a live game in highly immersive VR? Or would they want to figure out the best way their ads can appear not only compellingly, along the best sight lines, but also without intruding?

With the COVID-19 pandemic, a large number of live events got cancelled—sports, concerts, conferences, trade shows, and so on. Immediately, a lot of concerts have gone virtual. Typically, live events are watched at scale on TV and mostly in 2-D. If the VR production values and experiences are great, these events can be best enjoyed immersively, where consumers feel like they are in the midst of the action. When the content is rich and engaging, that is a powerful opportunity for brands to connect with their consumers. Today, many marketers have already discovered that simply taking a TV ad and shoving it into the digital channels is not the way to do it; it doesn't garner great results. In exactly the same way, marketers cannot simply take 2-D ads and slap them into a VR environment. They have to be appropriately native to VR in order to fit in and generate strong results.

In the not too distant future, we will see the emergence of VR-based trade shows and conferences, both for efficiency (cost and time) and impact. These shows and conferences will actually scale dramatically, even while giving remote participants a fully immersive and very realistic experience.

SMART SPEAKERS

Amazon, Google, and several others have started producing smart speakers. These are internet-connected speakers, where the user asks or gives commands verbally to the virtual assistant, which responds back in voice. The user's interaction with a smart speaker is predominantly, if not only, voice based. For example, if users ask a question to the smart speaker, addressing it "Alexa" or "Hey, Google," they get their answer. They search, they query, and they even make purchases. The whole interaction and purchase process is via voice, so we call it voice commerce. From searching to evaluating and purchasing, everything happens via voice.

Voice commerce is taking off in a big way. The smart speaker's interface is becoming smarter and smarter, and the voice is sounding more human and realistic. More and more people are buying these smart speakers. By the end of 2019, more than 25 percent of all households in the United States had a smart speaker.[4]

A company typically shows up in a traditional visual environment by showcasing its product in an appealing way and reinforcing the product with its brand, which is deeply researched and very well designed. This approach has evolved to become very scientific, and it has been working very well to help the company stand out of the clutter, grab consumers' attention, and hopefully motivate them enough to buy its product. But with smart speakers, everything is happening through voice. There is no visual real estate. And when there is no visual real estate, all the visual optimization done so far is made irrelevant for that context in one fell swoop.

So, brands need to figure out how to operate in this voice-only environment. It is important to note that, in a visual context, consumers can see multiple things at once. A brand can appear along with a bunch of other brands or other content on the same screen, at the same time. But audio is linear, sequential. One can talk about or hear about only one piece of content or one brand at a time. So, when a consumer searches, marketers must figure out how their brands show up as the first recommendation. It is also interesting to note that, according to a survey based study, 70 percent of all smart speaker owners have made at least one purchase via these devices.[5] So now there is a new gatekeeper/influencer/ quasi decision-maker in Alexa/Amazon. It will have an entirely new dynamic that marketers need to deal with.

HOLOGRAPHIC PROJECTION

A few years back, Tupac Shakur appeared magically on the stage at the Coachella Valley Music and Arts Festival concert. People went crazy. It was a quasi-holographic effect, in which videos were played and reflected by angled mirrors, giving the audience a reasonably realistic illusion. Since then, holograms have advanced a lot, and several companies are resurrecting dead singers who go on concert tours. So, brands that sponsor music concerts can now sponsor 3-D holographic tours of dead artists! I saw a demonstration of the concept with Roy Orbison and Maria Callas, and it felt authentic. There was a real orchestra onstage, and each singer's hologram, a very realistic one at that, was right in their midst, interacting with them and with the audience. It was fascinating. At that time, I had to sit right in front of the stage within a certain angle to get a realistic effect. And very real, it was!

Since then, Microsoft launched Mixed Reality powered by Azure AI. In an amazing demonstration, a presenter in Vegas showed how she could be virtually transported to and holographically projected in Japan to give a keynote there. Not only that, thanks to AI, the presenter, who did not speak Japanese, was made to look like she was actually speaking in Japanese, while fully being authentic in terms of her tone of voice, inflections, and so on. To the Japanese audience, it could look like this woman was there and making an excellent speech in Japanese—with no traveling or language lessons required. This could be game changing across multiple fields—from health care to entertainment to virtual meetings and more. Above all, it can provide incredible opportunities for marketing.[6]

Holographic concerts are here to stay. And they need sponsors. Since they will be competing with live concerts of living artists, there will be an overall surplus in supply that would hopefully keep the prices for those sponsorships low and affordable. But what's the consumers' bandwidth? How many concerts can they consume? For marketers, particularly those that are in the experiential space or considering being in the experiential space, this is an area that they must closely watch and strategize for the future.

Sales and product demos can be powerful and compelling when done via holographic projections. It is like being there with the customers with the product and showing them how exactly it works in amazing detail. This can evolve into a powerful B2B marketing and sales tool.

Other potential applications for holographic projections could range from ad co-creation sessions, customer service sessions, virtual showrooms, product training sessions for the salesforce, and so on.

To be at the top of their game, marketers need to stay on top of these kinds of developments, figure out what opportunities they can leverage these for, and come up with strategies to test, learn, refine, and launch.

THE INTERNET OF THINGS (IOT)

Every device at home and work, and those on the way, will be connected in the Fifth Paradigm. Every connected device could be a marketing medium. Home appliances, thermostats, home locks, cars, scales, suitcases, and on and on will all be gathering data, and many will even provide interfaces for interaction via voice or visual or both. Since every connected device gathers data, marketers need to be able to pull it all together, make sense out of it, arrive at actionable insights, and act upon them. It could be as simple as serving a personalized ad on the refrigerator screen (Samsung already has such a refrigerator with a screen),[7] or on the dashboard of a connected car or over its speakers.

This has a significant impact on how marketers organize and gear up their infrastructure and capabilities. The ad world has to rethink their entire architecture, the entire way ads are bid for and served in an IoT environment. Today, there is no such ecosystem or infrastructure to support it.

Marketers need to think about their consumer journey, identify either pain points or sales opportunities in real time, and take real-time action. This necessitates a total rethink of the current marketing and advertising approach, processes, and tech enablement.

WEARABLES

From watches, sneakers, head- and armbands to rings and clothes, wearables are already here, although highly fragmented. People are getting very taken in by the ability of these wearables to measure anything and everything about themselves, and the quest for the quantified self is moving forward quickly. Whether the wearables are connected in real time or by batch upload to the cloud, these devices gather vital information about consumers in areas that matter to them very much. (Hence, the reason they wear wearables in the first place!) So, what do marketers do with this data if indeed they can access it?

The implications are very similar to IoT, except that the data from wearables focuses on the areas that consumers want to know

about themselves and thus may offer more in-depth and unprecedented insights into individuals. I would always caution marketers
to be deeply respectful about consumers' privacy and not intrude
into their lives. Don't do anything without their explicit permission, and make sure they know in plain language what permission
they are giving, without hiding behind reams of legalese. The data
from wearables can offer a new layer of invaluable information for
product or offer development.

3-D PRINTING

3-D printing can be a boon for marketers in multiple industries—
from health care to automotive to industrial to financial. When you
look at the fourth P of marketing, it is all about place, i.e., distribution. 3-D printing can be a big opportunity and solution for distribution. Let me give you a few examples.

➤ **Health Care.** 3-D-printed, customized prosthetics or accesso-
ries, like hearing aids, will quickly become the norm in the Fifth
Paradigm. For instance, I know someone recently who had a fallen
arch in his foot and went to a foot surgeon. The surgeon suggested
some prosthetics, took measurements, and said it would be a few
weeks before he would receive them. How cool would it have been
if he was able to 3-D print the prosthetic then and there and give it
to my friend?

➤ **Automotive.** Customers get spare parts 3-D printed on-site.

➤ **Merchandise.** Merchandise or small product samples can be 3-D
printed.

➤ **Personalization.** 3-D printing gives a fantastic opportunity for
customization.

➤ **Product prototyping.** 3-D printing can help with product prototyping, getting it done faster and with much less expense than traditional methods of prototyping—whether a shampoo bottle or an industrial product.

Besides these, other technologies are advancing fast, like robotics and drones, that will impact the world of marketing and one or more of its 4 Ps.

Marketers need to understand the implications and opportunities of all these technology changes, prepare for that brave future, and leverage their power for their company or brand. How do they shape their engagement methodologies and material to be as multidimensional and as versatile as the media itself? These technologies, powered by AI and 5G, can enable amazing things: highly customized, contextually appropriate, personalized, engaging, interactive, and immersive solutions and experiences. Marketers can wow the consumers, without spooking them or freaking them out. The world ahead is one of phenomenal possibilities.

TO SUMMARIZE . . .

➤ There is going to be a new ecosystem that emanates from a combination of a barrage of new technologies. Marketers need to plan on how they will keep on top of and ahead of the evolution.

➤ How can they take advantage of these emerging new dimensions?

➤ What kind of partnerships do they need to establish to leverage and develop and test their initiatives in these new spaces?

➤ What are the costs and benefits and how can they begin testing these models and learning from the tests?

➤ Do they need internal talent to develop these solutions? If they rely on external partners, do they need to bring themselves and their teams up the curve via training or workshops?

CHAPTER 7

Unblocking the Blockchains

There is a lot of confusion in people's minds as to the difference between blockchains and Bitcoins. Many mistake them to be one and the same. But there is a huge difference between the two. Let me try to demystify blockchains.

Bitcoin is a currency. Blockchain is the technology that creates, tracks, and manages Bitcoins, and all the other cryptocurrencies, for that matter. At its simplest, blockchain is a virtual book for record keeping. In accounting terms, a book that keeps all the transaction records is called a ledger. Normally, an accountant or an accounting department enters the various transactions into a ledger and keeps it up to date. Blockchain is a digital ledger of transactions, with all the associated details. Did it happen? How much? When? What were the terms? While fundamentally the same, a blockchain is different. Instead of one person or department maintaining a ledger, it is distributed to or shared with a community, members of which make it their task to validate and timestamp these transactions. This is called a "distributed ledger."

There are many types of blockchain technologies, but generally speaking, whenever a transaction happens, the entire community gets to see it. That transaction is called a block. Once a block in the blockchain is created, it cannot be tampered with. It is called "immutable," and no one can alter the details. If someone adds incremental data or other content to the transaction, it shows up as a new block, in full view of all the participants. Therefore, because everyone in the community sees every block of the transaction, there is a high level of trust. And the proof of the transaction is cast in stone (well, a digital stone!). The proof of the transaction is irrefutable and the transaction details are immutable.

For many industries, blockchains can be very helpful in increasing transparency and reducing the complexity of transactions. For example, they can be extremely valuable in tracking produce supply chains. Say a contamination of some vegetable necessitates it being pulled off shelves. How does a company identify the source and pull everything from that batch or farm from all the shops? Tracking it with existing systems will take several days to try and figure out, if at all. With a blockchain, every stage of the vegetable's journey is clearly tracked, from the farm to the local warehouse to the vehicle that drove it into the city to the warehouse in that city and, finally, to the store shelf it made it to. Each stage is a block. And these blocks (or records) are immutable. Thanks to blockchains, it takes just a few seconds to trace the journey.

Bitcoin, on the other hand, is one type of cryptocurrency, the most widely known one. Cryptocurrencies are not issued or backed by any government. Their supply is kept limited, and depending on demand, people are willing to pay more or less, with their country's government-backed currency, for a given unit. The value of cryptocurrencies can fluctuate wildly, and at this time, it is a gambling game. Cryptocurrencies in general are enabled by blockchain technology.

Without going too much into cryptocurrencies, it is sufficient for us at this stage to know that:

➤ Bitcoin is a type of cryptocurrency; blockchain is a type of technology.

➤ Blockchain is the underlying technology for running cryptocurrencies.

➤ Cryptocurrencies are just one form among all the possible types of applications of blockchains.

➤ Blockchains are a system of record keeping, without a central authority or a single source of control. They are distributed to all the participants who stand witness to every transaction, which prevents such transactions from being tinkered with later on.

Before we dive into some examples from the marketing world, let's also address another term frequently mentioned in the context of blockchains. This term is *smart contract*. Let's say there are two parties (there can be multiple parties, but let's keep it simple). They agree to a deal or a transaction, with terms and conditions acceptable to both. These terms and conditions are then encoded into a software program that runs automatically and ensures their enforcement. This is called a smart contract. It is not "tinkerable"; you cannot change it. The parties involved can trust the transaction and its outcome, with no need for intermediaries to verify or validate. No one needs to weigh in to say that the transaction really happened as per the agreed terms and conditions, and nobody needs to reconcile any numbers later on. This is the core value of blockchains.

ADVERTISING PAYMENTS

The advertising ecosystem is opaque, filled with trust issues, allegations of kickbacks, fudging of data, and so on. The Association of National Advertisers (ANA) commissioned K2 Intelligence to study industry practices a few years back. Their findings were stunning— agency kickbacks from publishers were widespread.[1] Ad fraud was rampant. Likewise, studies showed that only 60 percent of ad dollars paid by a brand owner goes to the publisher. The rest goes to the intermediaries, whose job it is to count, verify, validate, and reconcile the numbers.[2] Between the brand owner and the publisher are a vast number of intermediaries at every stage who take their own piece of the pie. As can be seen from the visual below (see Figure 5), intermediaries include the media agency, the demand-side platform, the ad server, the ad exchange, the preverification platform, the supply-side platform, and the data validating/verification platforms. And this is just a subset of everyone who plays in this space.

ADVERTISING ECOSYSTEM

FIGURE 5

Clearly, when less than 60 percent of ad dollars goes to the publisher, it is high time for the value chain and the ecosystem to be fixed. And this is where blockchains can come in.

Advertisers should be paying only for those ads that have appeared legitimately and appropriately. They need to know that their ad was viewed by real human beings, not by bots. They need to know that their ad appeared on a real site, not a fraudulent site. They need to know that their ad was clearly viewable. They need to make sure that they get data back upon which they can make the payment. Because of the lack of trust, prevalence of fraud, and all the bad practices out there, they need a system they can trust and a system that brings in cost efficiencies by removing some intermediaries. They will still need some intermediaries, but there are opportunities to cut out a few layers.

With blockchain technology, brands can have smart contracts with the publishers and any essential intermediaries. Each party will gain access to the same information of real impressions, as defined and agreed upon a priori. They all can see what exactly is happening. And the advertiser can then pay for exactly what was delivered. They can save significant amounts of money, which can be put back into the business, instead of paying the intermediaries, or worse, paying for fraud.

Through blockchains, marketers can not only get cost advantage, but they also get the much-needed transparency and accuracy of data. And what's more, marketers can have a clearer picture of what is working and how well, so they can optimize their dollar allocation across various media channels or campaigns. When they have full transparency, they can make the right calls. In the absence of that, they may be optimizing, if it can be called that, based on incorrect information.

Blockchain is more secure than traditional accounting, since the records are distributed across all the parties. If any of the participants' systems get hacked, the data is still intact for the rest of the participants. To hack a ledger, the hacker has to hack every participant in the blockchain and every place where it is stored. That makes the decentralized way of keeping data far more secure than keeping it at a central place.

If blockchains are this good and this effective, surely they must be widely adopted in the ad space by now, right? Not exactly. Not everyone in the ecosystem stands to gain as does the advertiser and the publisher. For blockchain to really take root, scale will be critical; this means a big portion of the media publishers and advertisers have to come together to build the blockchain ecosystem. This is obviously not in the best interests of all the middlemen, because their roles and incomes will disappear. But this is eventually going to happen, as it must.

Some companies like IBM have done some pilots with Unilever and MediaOcean. Early results showed them that reclaiming fifteen to twenty cents on the dollar within the next five years is a reasonable goal. The global online advertising market is worth $333 billion this year, according to eMarketer. So, savings could run about $65 billion.[3]

In the Fifth Paradigm, marketers will be under even more pressure to find opportunities for efficiencies, even as they are expected to deliver results. Blockchains will play a key role.

THE REST OF THE MARKETING VALUE CHAIN

Like advertising value chains, there are other value chains in the world of marketing, such as the postproduction value chain, packaging value chain, promotional value chain, influencer value chain, and so on. There are opportunities across each one of these areas. The simple rule of thumb is this: any process with multiple intermediaries, concerns of transparency, deficit in trust, prevalence of fraud, need for validation or proof of transaction, and reconciliation of numbers is ripe for blockchains.

PROVENANCE

This is another word we often hear in the context of blockchains: *provenance*. Provenance is the ability to trace the origin of a product and tracking down its journey. This is very important for marketers, particularly for luxury goods, pharmaceuticals, and spare parts. Wherever there is a risk of spurious products being brought into the market, it's critical to know which is an authentic original and which is a fake. An item can be tracked from the point it is manu-factured until it reaches the buyer. At every stage, at every handoff from one part of the supply chain to the next, the product is vali-dated for authenticity. If a spurious product enters the market, it will not have this kind of an authenticated journey.

In the Third and Fourth Paradigms, companies that manufac-tured luxury goods would affix holograms to a product to demon-strate its authenticity. The assumption here was that it was extremely difficult, if not impossible, to duplicate the hologram. So, one can be fairly confident that the product with the hologram is the original one. In the Fifth Paradigm, digital IDs will be the equiv-alent of holograms. Each product will have a unique digital ID at-tached to it, and via the blockchain technology, it can be tracked all the way from the factory to the retail outlet and beyond.

In this day and age of trust deficits and persistent deceit, a seal of authenticity could be a huge brand differentiator. That is exactly what the combination of blockchain and digital ID can bring to the table. Let's say a consumer is in the market for a Patek Philippe watch. The consumer needs to track its ownership history to have solid evidence of authenticity. Blockchain with its provenance ca-pability is the answer.

Also, for many people, the origin of their food is very important. When consumers see an organic product on a retail shelf, for in-stance, they may want to see where and when it was produced, where it traveled before reaching the store, and so on. The concept of provenance does exactly that. For those who are environmentally conscious, or sensitive to manufacturing practices, wanting to know the origin and the journey of a product, blockchain will be an invaluable technology. In future, consumers' sensitivities will be at an all-time high and the burden of proof of authenticity will be on the brands.

There can be so many opportunities to leverage blockchains within marketing. In the Fifth Paradigm, blockchains will truly get unblocked and will become fairly core to the entire marketing ecosystem.

TO SUMMARIZE . . .

➤ Blockchains are not the same as Bitcoins or other crypto-currencies. Blockchains are the underlying technology for cryptocurrencies.

➤ Blockchains bring substantial value in terms of trust, transparency, and immutability to transactions in an ecosystem via smart contracts.

➤ Blockchains can bring efficiencies and much-needed trust back into the advertising value chain. It has potential application in other marketing value chains as well.

➤ Provenance is an important concept that helps track the journey and the origin of any item, which has many applications around product authenticity, product journey, and source credibility in the marketing world.

CHAPTER 8

The Sciences behind Marketing

During one of my international stints, I was having dinner with one of my senior colleagues, who was an MBA and spent the earlier part of his career in marketing. He later went on to become a successful general manager. He made a very interesting point that evening. So long as you get your 4 Ps right and a half-decent ad campaign developed and launched to tell your product story, you have done successful marketing. Why, he asked, do we need to over-complicate marketing?

At a high level, he wasn't wrong. But the key question is—how do you get to that right marketing mix? How do you create the right product with the right attributes and benefits? How do you price it in a way that works for the consumer and the company? How do you know what kind of package evokes what kinds of feelings and actions from the consumer? How do you know how to create that campaign, half decent or wholly compelling? How do you even know that your offering has staying power and is not a one-and-done wonder? You can't create a successful mix based solely on intuition or even by deploying rudimentary methodologies. There are sciences behind each of these aspects that help the marketer gain powerful insights that will lead to successful outcomes.

One of the tenets of Quantum Marketing is to integrate the power of art, technology, and science to get into the consumers' heads and hearts. The goal is to learn how and why consumers think, feel, and act in any given way and how to influence their preferences.

Substantial developments are happening in the world of science, though not as rapidly as in the case of technology. Nevertheless, these scientific developments have a profound impact on market-ing. Marketing has always relied on several sciences—psychology, sociology, anthropology, mathematics, and more. But areas like be-havioral economics, neuroscience, sensorial science (study of sight, sound, smell, taste, and touch), and the science of anonymity have started complementing the traditional sciences. They are driving marketing to an entirely different level.

Let's look at a few of them.

BEHAVIORAL ECONOMICS (BE)

Behavioral economics is not a new science. It has been around since the early 1970s, and luminaries like Daniel Kahneman and Richard Thaler have brought the field into prominence and commercial limelight. Simply put, behavioral economics is the study of how various factors, such as psychological, emotional, or social influ-ence, affect the economic decisions of individuals and institutions. This is one of the most engaging fields and is fun to learn about.

We use BE to find better ways of deciphering how consumers will behave, as opposed to their intent, in the face of alternatives. Their decisions cannot be explained based only on traditional, ra-tional economic models or logic. Why do consumers sometimes buy a less financially attractive option when presented with a superior alternative?

It all boils down to the way individuals process, think, feel, and then decide. All of this is affected by psychological, emotional, social, and cultural factors. When we integrate the insights from across all these fields, we realize that there is a method to the madness, after all. Behavioral economics can give us frameworks to understand the relationships and interrelationships of various parameters in the face of which consumers make choices. The application of behavioral economics is coming to the fore, not only in business-to-consumer marketing but also in business-to-business marketing.

Let me give an overly simplistic example. Say we present a consumer two different offers: two $100 jackets for $150 or the first jacket for $100 and the second for only $50. Simple arithmetic shows that both offer the exact same value. Rational theory would suggest that the consumer would treat the two offers the same and each offer would perform identically. But, in reality, more people may be more likely to take the second offer. This has a profound impact on how marketers set prices and design promotions.

It is absolutely essential that marketers have a very good understanding of how to optimize and construct their promotions and campaigns. Many promotions can be tested and verified through experimental techniques. It's very expensive and time consuming to do these studies, however, and it is practically impossible to test every single promotion. This is even more so in a real-time marketing scenario.

When we study behavioral economics, we come up with solid frameworks, parameters, and paradigms to predict consumer choices based on limited tests and experiments. We can then refine these hypotheses and models as we go along, in real time. In addition, AI is set to enter the field and bring in a new depth in understanding decision dynamics so we can prognosticate with precision.

Let's take another example. Marketers are deciding on a pricing strategy for a watch that will include a promotional discount. In the first approach, they price the watch at $400 and give 10 percent off. The net price to the consumer is $360. In the second approach, they jack up the price to $500 and give a 20 percent discount. The net price to the consumer in this case is $400, $40 more than in the first approach. Assume the major competing brand is priced at $450 and has exactly the same functionality, quality, and brand stature. Which approach is better? Or should the marketer just price it at parity with the competitor, because there is more revenue to be made that way?

Financially and logically speaking, the first route is more attractive to the consumer, so one would think that that it would result in gaining substantial market share and creating a good sales momentum. Right? Not so fast! Should the marketers do a price test, A-B testing, experimental design, factor analysis, or something else? All those will give some insights to some level but probably fewer insights into the reasons why. BE would look into this and get an excellent grasp of the interrelationships and interactions between the things that influence choice. In this example, the pricing at $500 creates a reference point against which $400 looks like a bargain, and it might actually end up being the more successful promotion.

Even relatively older theories (from 1899) like those of Thorstein Veblen can be very insightful and add to the depth of thinking around pricing and promotional strategies. For example, luxury goods are often bought and displayed rather conspicuously to signal the status of the buyer. The Veblen effect says that the demand for these kind of products goes up as the price increases, because the higher price signals to the consumer that the intrinsic value or the status factor is better. This is the exact opposite of what classical microeconomic theories say—that price and demand are inversely correlated.

Ravi Dhar, professor at Yale University and the director of its Center for Customer Insights, is right when he says, "Most marketers assume that consumers are rational agents who weigh each option carefully considering all possible trade-offs, whereas in practice choices emerge out of intuitive processing that makes some option look more attractive than others."

Whenever consumers have competing choices, how do they choose? How do marketers understand how they make those choices? And how do marketers leverage that understanding and those insights into how they craft their future campaigns and promotions? How will it affect pricing strategies or even the positioning of brands and products? How and why do consumers respond to different packages differently, when everything else is kept the same? Behavioral economics could provide some of the answers, which can significantly help marketers shape better strategies.

NEUROSCIENCE

The earliest known medical text, describing a brain injury in 1600 BCE, showcases our interest in the brain.[1] So our desire to understand the brain is not exactly new. With modern advances, neuroscience is gaining more of a foothold now than ever before, as we are approaching the Fifth Paradigm.

When we conduct research for new ads, packaging, and so on, traditionally we ask consumers what they like and why. We assume that when consumers say they like a product, packaging, or an ad, they have observed all the details and then they liked it. Likewise, we assume that they state what exactly they like, and truly understand why they like what they like. In reality, many consumer feelings, including liking something or not, happen more subconsciously and almost spontaneously. In other words, they may not know what they like and know even less why they like what they say they like. Ninety percent of decision-making takes place in the subconscious. By definition, the subconscious is "sub" (meaning below) conscious awareness. If we rely only on conscious tools that involve asking people questions or moving a dial, we will miss out on important information that is driving consumer behavior. Neuroscience is extremely helpful in bringing order to this space. In studies, scientists put on a person a shower-cap-like headset that has nonintrusive electrodes or sensors on the underside. These sensors detect electrical impulses in the brain as they happen. When a particular pattern of brain activity occurs—such as greater activity in the left frontal cortex compared to the right frontal cortex—it may clearly indicate that the consumer likes what they have just seen. And if the opposite occurs, it might signal that the consumer felt negatively about it.

Now show the consumer a video ad. As the ad progresses, the brain starts lighting up in different areas as the neurons fire and different parts of the brain communicate. The headset helps track the brain activity second by second and maps that activity to every part of the ad. So, at the end of the study, marketers know exactly which parts of the ad the consumers found interesting and positive, which parts they were indifferent to, which parts they were turned off by, which parts of the ad they were likely to remember, and so on. Note that measurement of subconscious memory differs from the traditional measures of conscious recall and retention. This is a wealth of information for any marketer to be able to act on to enhance the ad's overall effectiveness.

According to Pranav Yadav, founder and CEO of Neuro-Insight: "While emotion is an important element of every story, the only thing that makes an ad effective is its 'long-term memory,' specifically at the point of branding and key messages. If you don't remember the key messages or branding moments in the ad, you're not going to act on the message in the market. Traditionally we've neither been able to measure actual 'long-term memory' nor have we had a second-by-second measure to pinpoint how we received branding or key messages, and we certainly have not been able to take the context (TV show or Instagram feed) into account. To be able to get this level of granularity is a huge breakthrough for brands."

Other similar techniques fall under the category of "biometrics," with different degrees of effectiveness. For example, facial encoding, eye tracking, and skin conductivity are easy to implement, and while they may not directly measure the brain, they can bring in a deeper layer of information and insights compared to traditional market research, both qualitatively and quantitatively.

SENSORIAL SCIENCE

The application of the science of senses in the field of marketing is relatively nascent, and I will cover it in detail in the next chapter, "All the Senses." The broad summary is this: it is becoming increasingly important (and is a huge opportunity for marketers) to leverage all five senses, to be able to cut through the clutter, engage consumers, and influence their choices and purchase decisions. Effective orchestration of the senses can be done to stimulate those parts of the brain that would help accomplish all this. This is an emerging field, and a lot of good work has begun in this space.

THE SCIENCE OF ANONYMITY

Strictly speaking, this is not exactly a science by itself, but I chose to include it here, given the significant role it can play and how much more is yet to be uncovered in this field. People behave differently when they are by themselves versus when they are in groups or social settings. An individual might be stingy when alone but may loosen the purse strings when in a group—just to feel a part of that group. And when anonymous, an individual can behave very differently still, whether alone or in a group. The anonymity reduces or eliminates inhibition and gives incremental confidence for people to do or say things they would not dare to do or say when their identities are known. Moreover, in an anonymous social setting, the additional layer of groupthink is at play as well. There is an amplification of boldness, aggression, and other behaviors.

How does anonymity affect consumer behavior and how does it, therefore, affect marketers? I will touch upon three important areas:

1. Online purchases don't give anonymity to consumers in the truest sense of the word, but it does remove them from physical contact. That changes behavior. For example, in conservative cultures, buying intimacy products or feminine hygiene products is a very awkward moment people would rather avoid. But when they have an online option, while not anonymous, they have a degree of separation, and they buy. So, online is the first degree of separation that can stimulate a purchase. Would marketers be able to drive both demand and preference if they more deeply understood the dynamics of anonymity? Yes. And I am not talking merely of removing the friction from making impulse purchases (which, of course, does push the demand up).

2. The second degree of separation, in which complete anonymity is provided, is the use of cryptocurrencies. When consumers buy something with, say, Bitcoins, they are assured that nobody can trace that purchase back to them. As a result, a lot of trafficking of drugs, pornography, and so on happens via such currencies. In fact, at one point, the combination of cryptocurrency and Silk Road, the website for everything nefarious, was deadly.

Marketers need to ask some pertinent questions and examine the answers for their product or service category. For example, if people want to buy something legally, but want to do it anonymously for whatever their personal reasons are, how does that purchase behavior manifest? Likewise, how would a pricing strategy using cryptocurrencies work? If marketers price in cryptocurrencies, would that endear them to their consumers? Or would they be assuming the volatility risk of the cryptocurrency and open themselves to potentially losing their shirts with one big move in the market? There are pros and cons to each approach, but marketers have to carefully think through them in their context and act thoughtfully.

3. In an anonymous social setting, people tend to be nastier and negative. A 2016 study led by Christopher Bartlett of Gettysburg College surveyed college students and found that, over the course of an academic year, people who felt that their identity was concealed online were more likely to report engaging in cyberbullying and holding positive attitudes toward cyberbullying. ("It's okay if someone deserves it.")[2]

In an anonymous setting, people tend to throw stones at brands more boldly and very generously. And in a situation of groupthink and communal piling on, how do marketers defend their brands? Social media is becoming all consuming, device addiction is becoming toxic, interpersonal interactions are changing, and the cultural fabric of our society is altering. Studying the science behind all of that is very important, because it will inform how marketers play their role in presenting and protecting their brands. When they better understand the underlying psychology and dynamics, they will be able to strategize and be better prepared. Research in this specific space and application is fairly nascent, but we will have a wealth of important insights in the not too distant future.

At another level, marketers also have to evaluate the role social media platforms assume in containing such adverse and, very often, unfair activity against brands. Should we urge social media platforms to be places where brands are safe and not trolled by the anonymous goons? After all, marketers fund the social platforms via their ad revenues, so should we not hold them accountable to prevent and mitigate brand bullying?

In the end, as much as we are focusing on the rapidly transforming technology landscape, we should not forget the basic sciences that affect marketing and the new developments taking place. Successful marketing begins with a deep understanding of the sciences and a deep adoption of the technology.

TO SUMMARIZE . . .

➤ Various fields of science are evolving in terms of their application to the marketing world. They enable a critical part of understanding the consumer in the Fifth Paradigm. Behavioral economics, neurosciences, and sensorial sciences have started complementing the classical frameworks. They are driving marketing to an entirely different level.

➤ As consumers deal with the barrage of marketing messages and other interactions, we cannot explain their decisions purely based on traditional economics or logic. Behavioral economics is searching for better ways of finding out how consumers will behave in the face of alternatives.

➤ Psychology, especially in anonymous environments, has a direct implication on social media dynamics. When marketers better understand the underlying psychology and the dynamics of behavior under anonymity, they will be better prepared for the inevitable social media roller-coaster ride.

CHAPTER 9

All the Senses

At this point, we're going to leave science and technology behind to focus on consumer dynamics and some of the other changes that will take place in the Fifth Paradigm, and how marketers should address and leverage them.

With a plethora of new devices, screens, and engaging and immersive content, information overload for an already overloaded consumer is going to be even more humungous. Consumers will simply be unable to process the things being thrown at them. They will deal with this by either tuning out, blocking out, or seeking refuge in paid, no-ad environments. While consumers will be easily accessible, their hearts and minds will be difficult to reach through the massive clutter. Yet marketers have to tell consumers their story—whether it is about their products, services, or brands.

How to do that? In a word: *senses*. First, let's look at some background before we learn about one of the most innovative developments in Quantum Marketing, i.e., Multisensory Marketing.

HOW OUR BRAIN FUNCTIONS

Our five senses constantly supply information to our brain. Different parts of the brain process this information and help us make sense of the world around us. Let's focus on just a couple of the parts and processes that have a direct bearing on and relevance to marketing.

First, there's the area traditionally termed the *primal brain*. The primal brain functions rapidly and with little effort. For example, when you see a tiger, you don't think; you just run. That is your reflex action. Your primal brain senses the danger, you feel intense fear, your adrenaline is pumped up, and you run for your life.

Feelings largely originate in the primal brain, which is also the seat of emotions. The primal brain has been identified with "System 1 thinking," the fast, seemingly effortless, subconscious, and intuitive thinking that guides much of our behavior and decision-making.

Second is the cognitive brain, which relates to what is termed System 2 thinking. The cognitive brain carefully analyzes the information and situation, and the result of that analysis drives the person to act or react in a particular way.

Most of our decisions are driven by what we feel, that is System 1 thinking. The cognitive brain might inform the decision, but the decision is driven by the feel. Let us take an example. If a consumer sees a label on a food product that reads "6 grams of protein," the processing of that information happens more rationally, through System 2. Its price, too, is evaluated through System 2. System 1, however, does the job of "reading between and behind the lines" subconsciously. The words, fonts, colors, shape, or imagery trigger or convey deeper and subtle meanings to us, based on our own experiences, eventually driving our purchase decision.

Marketers need to focus on the feel and nonverbal aspects a whole lot more, I would daresay, than on the rational aspect. Anatomically, the parts of the brain that process scents are located close to the hippocampus where the brain stores memories. Scents, therefore, evoke the strongest memories. Messages can be conveyed to consumers by vision, sound, taste, smell, or touch. Millions of data points are stored in our memories without our conscious awareness, and if marketers use the right visuals and symbols, music and rhythm, texture and touch, fragrances and flavors, they can resonate more deeply than mere rational claims.

Typically, when marketers think of an ad, they think of a static ad, audio ad, or an audiovisual ad. Irrespective of what type of ads or through what modes, the most impactful ads are those that primarily cue the right associations through System 1 thinking, probably even to the exclusion of the cognitive brain. If marketers tap into the appropriate subconscious associations (e.g., trust, reliability, innovation) effectively with their campaigns, they get the most results. Additional components that appeal to the rational cognitive brain can be the icing on the cake.

In traditional marketing, marketers rely predominately on sight and sound. In Quantum Marketing, they need to address and leverage as many of the five senses as possible. All five collectively can provide tremendous impact. This is what we refer to as multisensory branding and Multisensory Marketing.

Sound, especially rhythm and music, addresses the primal part of the brain, where it immediately translates to feelings, emotions, and sometimes movement. Furthermore, consumers are biologically forced to listen to any sound that is playing (we can't just choose to not hear something), whereas they can simply look away from any visual. Unless people have earplugs in, sound always grabs their attention, making it a very powerful way into their hearts and minds.

This sound can take many forms: music, voices of the narrator and characters, ambient sounds, and so forth. One big leap in how we will leverage sound in the Fifth Paradigm is to create the equivalent of a visual brand logo and design system in the audio space. We call it sonic branding. There would be a whole series of sounds that would come to uniquely define and distinguish a brand.

Branding is a critical part of marketing. And sonic branding is a critical extension of the overall branding, a key element of

Quantum Marketing. Sonic branding is not just about having nice background music or a jingle. It is the creation of a comprehensive sonic brand architecture, pretty much like marketers have a visual brand architecture today. Just as a brand typically has a logo and a design system that people associate it with, marketers need to create a sonic brand identity that people can instantly recognize.

In earlier marketing paradigms, we used to have jingles to create strong associations between a tune and the brand. Though that approach is unidimensional, jingles have been very effective. I, as most of you do, too, still remember from my childhood the jingles of several brands I either loved or hated, but certainly never ignored. Today, marketers need to go way beyond jingles.[1]

Mastercard's case study of its sonic brand creation is instructive.[2] We created a comprehensive sonic brand architecture starting with the creation of a thirty-second melody. This is the core DNA of the sonic brand, a collection and sequence of notes that create a tune that is, first and foremost, very pleasant. Obviously, we didn't want the brand to be associated with an unpleasant tune. The melody had to be:

➤ **Memorable**—because the connection between a melody and the brand doesn't happen unless the melody is memorable.

➤ **Hummable**—so it sticks deeper in people's memories. It becomes something that is unpleasantly called an ear worm. In reality, it is a sound or a tune that lodges in your mind in a very positive way.

➤ **Neutral**—because it should be supportive and appropriate to any situation or message, as opposed to dominating and drowning everything else out.

➤ **Versatile across cultures**—because, as universal as music is, it manifests quite differently from country to country, region to region, and culture to culture. So, we wanted to make sure that this melody ported beautifully across cultures and continents.

➤ **Adaptable and appropriate to different genres**—because whether people are listening to classical opera or electronic dance music, whether at a country music festival or a rock concert, the melody has to be totally at home.

➤ **Appropriate to any situation**—be it an energetic soccer match or a beautiful and mellow romantic evening, at a high-decibel night club or somewhere solemn or nostalgic—the melody has to be totally adaptable.

When this brief was given to the music agencies, I still remember the looks on their faces—total bewilderment and truly priceless expressions!

After two years of intense work with musicians, musicologists, composers, studios, and various artists, we managed to come up with just such a melody. In the words of Mike Shinoda, a terrific musician and a cofounder of Linkin Park, this melody is so simple yet so unique that a small adjustment in tempo or instrumentation immediately transports it into a different culture.

This melody is part of every one of Mastercard's ads, as the background or foreground music. It is played at all Mastercard events and forums. We play this when people calling Mastercard offices are placed on hold. We even made ring tones out of it, literally dozens of them, that anyone can download. The melody of Mastercard has been extremely well tested to make sure that it is validated by neurological studies, which found it to be evocative: it is pleasant, it is hummable, it is memorable, and it is highly adaptable to any situation, any genre, any culture. Therefore, people can relate to it and like it in any part of the world, in any situation. It truly feels native to every situation it is put in.

THE TAXONOMY OF SONIC BRANDING

While the melody is the first and foundational level of the brand architecture, a subset of this melody, three seconds long, is the signature (see Figure 6). One of the best examples of sonic signature is that of Intel, where every ad is signed off with its extremely well-known sonic mnemonic. What is unique in Mastercard's sonic signature is its derivation from the melody. By maintaining a firm connection to its root melody, and thereby working together with the sonic melody, it reinforces Mastercard's sonic identity.[3]

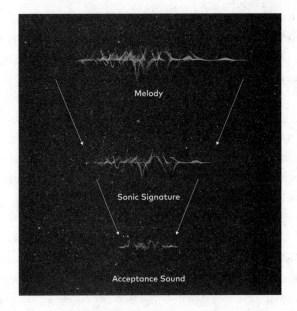

FIGURE 6

Every Mastercard advertisement will end with this sonic signature. This is the second level of sonic branding, and we looked for more opportunities to populate it. For example, all the company PCs and laptops play the sonic signature when they start up.

Then there is a third level: a further subset of our sonic melody, measuring 1.3 seconds. It is embedded into the physical and digital points of all interaction with Mastercard. We call this our acceptance sound. Every time a payment transaction goes through successfully, consumers will hear the reassuring sound of Mastercard. At the time of this writing, the Mastercard acceptance sound is already incorporated into more than fifty million points of interaction around the world and marching forward strongly.

To get universal recognition for our brand logo, we have consistently invested in the brand-building effort for more than five decades. That's what has made the logo recognizable around the world, even without the name Mastercard on it. In fact, we dropped our name from our logo at the beginning of 2019, making it one of the few iconic symbol brands.[4]

But to achieve that level of recognition for the sonic brand, we don't want to, and can't, wait another five decades. So how do we build that universal awareness rapidly? We evolved a strategy called the 3 As—awareness, association, and attribution. The *awareness* of the melody needs to be built first. Then, once people recognize it, they need to start *associating* it with Mastercard, which means they will start making the connection between the sound and the brand. And finally, they will be able to correctly *attribute* it to Mastercard, over a period of time.

How do we create a strong awareness? We cannot just keep playing our melody over and over in our ads and videos. We decided to create our own original music, with the Mastercard melody subtly infused into it. The key point here is subtlety. If any, or worse, every song sounds like a corporate anthem, people will recoil. We need to be delicate. The brand melody needs to be beautifully and naturally intertwined with each song. And so we began our journey and launched our first pop song, called "Merry Go Round,"[5] at the beginning of 2020. We have partnered with world-class talent. Next in line is the launch of a full music album, naturally named *Priceless!*

At the end of the very first year since its launch, Mastercard's sonic brand was recognized as the best in the world, leaping ahead of a number of other brands that have had brand sounds for decades.[6]

THE SENSE OF TASTE

In addition to visual and sonic brand strategies, Mastercard also embarked on a journey to tap into the sense of taste. Taste has a very close connection to the primal brain. It affects consumers rapidly. For the most part, people tend to like or dislike a taste instantaneously. And if they don't like something instantly, it can take them a long time to acquire a taste for it.

Taste is very natural to a brand associated with edible products or drinks. But what about brands like Mastercard that do not have any natural reason to be associated with taste? Well, we could come out with edible prepaid cards, but that's probably not a smart idea. Instead, Mastercard launched a program called Priceless Tables, where a fabulous dinner is served at a table or two set up in exotic and completely unexpected places—like on top of a billboard in Manhattan or next to a dinosaur skeleton in a Chicago museum or on a baseball diamond.[7] These tables, thousands of which we created around the world, create a terrific experience for the consumers, at scale. And they directly result in a brand image uplift, with a lot of conversations about it in social media.

We even launched restaurants, including in Manhattan. Some of these restaurants, by design, are faithful re-creations of exotic restaurants from around the world. And we keep changing the themes to keep the concepts fresh. For example, one of the restaurants, called The Rock, was a very exotic restaurant that stands literally on a rock, off the coast of Zanzibar in Tanzania. We replicated the restaurant to a T, including the view from each window to be exactly the same as if the diner were in the original restaurant. The menu, the sea breeze, the fragrance, the specially composed background music leveraging our sonic melody—it created a stunning multisensory experience. The idea was to create such wholesome, multisensory experiences that money cannot buy—only a Mastercard can bring them to you.[8]

Mastercard has even created macarons in unique flavors in partnership with Ladurée, the premier French baker. One flavor is the taste of optimism, the second, the taste of passion, and they are presented in the two colors of the Mastercard logo, red and yellow. Sold through select Ladurée stores, they are also given to Mastercard clients at various events and conferences to reinforce the brand through their taste buds.[9]

Another excellent example of multisensory branding comes from Aston Martin, the iconic British carmaker, famously associated with James Bond. This brand has done some amazing work in the multisensory space. As a luxury brand, its sales volumes are naturally limited and similarly don't have gigantic marketing budgets. So, rather than relying on traditional marketing, they explored new fields to make their brand impact felt. One such direction is sensorial marketing, including sonic branding.

Unsurprisingly for a brand that has been around for more than a hundred years, the sonic identity has been built over many decades and at its heart is the distinctive sound of the engine. The exhaust note is the rumble of the car, a carefully engineered soundtrack that can switch from mellow to malevolent with a squeeze of the throttle. Nothing has been left to chance to ensure that every sound the car makes is in harmony with the engine sound, from the seat belt alerts and low fuel reminders, to the particular click of the gearshift and the soft creak of the leather upholstery.

Each element of the sonic identity, no matter how insignificant, has been given much thought. Using the fasten seat belt tone as an example, Aston Martin decided to make the warning more melodic, to be suggestive rather than demanding. If the driver ignores it, there is a second and a third transition in intensity to convey the urgency. The fundamentals of sonic identity are matching the sounds the car makes to the visual identity of the brand. Sounds that express and encapsulate the craftsmanship, refinement, and unique character of the brand.

Aston Martin also has deployed the other senses of touch and smell. It takes more than a hundred hours to craft the interior of an Aston Martin and it is all done to deliver a sensory experience, from the unique touch sensation when a customer runs her fingers over the leather interior to the aroma of the leather. The aroma is so distinctive that when Aston Martin Works restores a vintage Aston Martin, they will source the leather from the original supplier to ensure the aroma of the leather is authentic to that car. Talk of being obsessed, in a great way, to being true to and consistent with every aspect of the brand manifestation.

Gerhard Fourie, Director of Marketing and Brand Strategy of Aston Martin, says "The identity of the brand has developed over many decades, and even when we move into new fields of marketing, it is essential that we maintain the essence of the brand. And to do so, we go to extraordinary lengths."

A number of other companies have been on the multisensory branding journey, albeit just getting started. Hotel chains, in particular Marriott, have been using "signature scents" as part of their branding campaign for many years.[10] Many retailers also take a similar approach, using scent to engage the brain's limbic system—the part most connected to memory and behavior.

Nike has found that when they added scents to its stores, purchase intent among customers increased by up to 80 percent. In a similar report, a gas station minimart in the UK found that the smell of coffee in the air increased their sales by 300 percent.[11] However, this should not be confused with sonic branding. Merely adding fragrances to enhance the consumer experience or stimulate their brain or evoke their feelings is not sensory branding. It is just sensory stimulation. Sensory branding is where the sounds, smells, taste, touch, etc., are all unique to that brand and are recognizable and uniquely associated with that brand. It is a brand identity creation, across multiple senses.

Multisensory branding is all about reaching consumers through all their senses in ways that are relevant, authentic, compelling, and nonintrusive, thus cutting through the massive clutter and reaching the consumers' hearts and minds.

TO SUMMARIZE . . .

➤ In an increasingly cluttered environment, marketers need to cut through that clutter and connect with the consumers through all five senses.

➤ In a world of smart speakers, the Internet of Things, and wearables, brands need to show up in sound, as there is no visual real estate in those environments.

➤ Sonic branding is a comprehensive brand identity with a clear architecture, not a mere jingle or mnemonic.

➤ Multisensory Marketing is a very important tenet of Quantum Marketing.

CHAPTER 10

Loyalty Transformed

I recently read something on BBC.com that made me sit up straight. According to the article, 75 percent of men and 68 percent of women admitted to cheating in some way, at some point in a relationship.[1] I thought that the number could probably have been around 30 percent. Fifty percent tops. But 75 percent?

I found that research was fairly sparse in this area, and the numbers for infidelity ranged anywhere from 30 to 60 percent in other studies. Studies have also indicated that the probability of a marriage ending in divorce is from 50 to 60 percent. These numbers are similar across the globe, despite people taking serious marriage vows and knowing of even more serious consequences. After all, people declare their loyalty "till death do us part." In some cases, they make a supreme being their witness. In some cases, the marriage is sanctified by mantras.

People know they pay a huge price if caught philandering outside marriage. In addition to the reputational implications, there could be deep financial ones. The emotional trauma for them and their near ones is significant. The price of disloyalty is steep.

Still, knowing all this, a vast majority don't seem to remain loyal. Is it because people are hardwired *not* to be loyal?

Asked another way, if people are not loyal in their committed relationships, are we as marketers and businesspeople realistic in expecting loyalty from our consumers? If they are not loyal in their personal lives, are we fantasizing that we will generate their loyalty to our brands? We are, after all, way down the food chain of attention, as far as people's lives are concerned. Are we missing the point here? Do we need to reimagine loyalty?

WHAT IS LOYALTY?

Let's go to the very basics. What is loyalty? According to Webster, *loyalty* implies a faithfulness that is steadfast in the face of any temptation to renounce, desert, or betray. Its synonyms are: piety, fidelity, allegiance, fealty, devotion.

In common parlance, we use these as fairly interchangeable words with very similar meanings, but they do have nuances that bring out beautifully the totality of the concept of loyalty.

Piety means faithfulness to something to which one is bound by pledge or duty. *Fidelity* implies strict and continuing faithfulness to an obligation, trust, or duty. *Allegiance* suggests an adherence like that of citizens to their country. *Fealty* implies a fidelity acknowledged by the individual and is as compelling as a sworn vow. *Devotion* stresses zeal and service amounting to self-dedication.

Collectively, they connote the concept of one's committed, dedicated, unwavering relationship to someone or something. For example, people may have an allegiance to a city and scream with joy when a singer shouts out its name at a concert. But that doesn't prevent them moving to other cities and calling them home. And then they begin fiercely supporting their new city. Likewise, people have strong feelings for their countries, even stronger than to their cities. But, for better opportunities, they move, change their citizenships, and build new affinities and allegiances to their adopted countries.

In the spectrum of their lives, people have stronger feelings of affiliation, allegiance, and loyalty to certain aspects more than others. For example, some are fiercely loyal to their sports team or to their political party or to a cause they deeply care about. Essentially, these are their passions. A person may be passionate about many areas, like music, sports, philanthropy, arts, culture, and so on. In all such passion areas, they exhibit strong feelings of affiliation or allegiance. And it is all totally voluntary. And in the event they do switch their allegiance, it is barely called out.

Now let's get back to marriage. While the act of getting into a marriage or a relationship is voluntary, it is expected to be a commitment. Marriage or a relationship typically demands exclusivity, in the face of every competing opportunity. In an area like sports, while people might be loyal fans of a particular team, they may also follow multiple sports and multiple teams; there is no implied or emotional exclusivity. Not so with marriage.

The hypothesis here is that human beings are not singularly loyal. And there is a fascinating hierarchy of loyalty at work, which I will cover a little later in this chapter.

It's time for brands to think about this. As I alluded to earlier, if people are not loyal to their own spouses, shouldn't we be asking ourselves why they would be loyal to our brands? Interestingly, across categories, consumers on average belong to fifteen loyalty programs. But only 25 percent actually use them. And only 22 percent see themselves as brand loyal. Just as 75 percent of people cheat on human relationships, pretty much the same number cheat on their brands.[2]

Does it mean that loyalty platforms and programs are useless? Far from it. In fact, just the opposite. Because of the non-loyalty factor, if consumers are with your competitors, you can win them over. And likewise, at every moment of truth, a brand risks losing a consumer, even if that consumer has been with the brand for a long time. Loyalty programs need to evolve and play a key role at every moment of consumer choice, while taking into consideration the consumer mind-set and leveraging those insights.

Loyalty programs will need to evolve from looking at the "winning and keeping consumers" mind-set to winning each transaction, building on the previous win. The goal will be to win a "higher share of preference" in favor of one's own brand. Consumers don't mind leaning more toward one brand, but when there are temptations and opportunities at hand, they do stray. For example, if we look at store loyalty programs, a consumer may belong to Costco, but that doesn't mean that she doesn't have the loyalty cards from Kroger or subscribe to and buy groceries from Amazon Prime. While winning some loyalty to a brand is a worthwhile goal, it's not reasonable for a brand to demand, expect, or get exclusivity.

In fact, brand loyalty reminds me of some of the hippie communes we saw in the '60s and '70s in the United States, India, and Europe. All the residents and their gurus were all about free love and a lack of commitment to any particular lifestyle. And that's exactly what they got. That lack of commitment meant any relationship at any time was without condition or consequence. It's a lot like today's consumer in the Fifth Paradigm. Why stay loyal when there's so much choice to be sampled?

Let's take another angle: we say that the customer is king or queen. That is a good attitude, since it is the customer who pays our salaries. Many brands have recognized this for a long time, so much so that they would proudly proclaim "our customer is king" or "the customer is always right!" But if the customer is the king or the queen, who should be loyal to whom? Is the king loyal to his subjects or are the subjects expected to be loyal to the king? Well, it is always the subjects (brands) who owe fealty, who, to borrow a line from *Game of Thrones*, "bend the knee." By that approach, we as marketers and companies have to rethink our approach to loyalty.

Before we move on to show how to craft a new approach in the Quantum Marketing framework, here's a quick summary:

➤ Brand exclusivity is an unrealistic aspiration.

➤ Brands/companies should recognize that consumers expect them to be loyal to them, not the other way around.

➤ Marketers need to understand the true dynamics of loyalty and healthy consumer relationships.

WHAT IS THE QUANTUM MARKETING APPROACH?

Now, all this is not to say that brands should throw brand equity programs away and head straight for deep discounts and private labels. Hardly. We can make marketing work for high-value as well as high-frequency purchases. First, understand what I call the hierarchy of loyalty (see Figure 7).

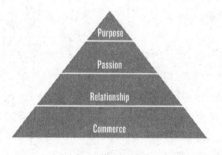

FIGURE 7

Loyalty is a continuum with four manifestations:

1. Purpose- or Cause-Driven. This is the highest order of commitment. When consumers can support a cause such as climate change, education, income equality, or medical research, they will do so with efforts and attitudes that transcend any selfish motive or any expectation of something in return. They care about something deeply and they support it fully. And they remain committed to that cause or purpose.

2. Passion-Driven. Go to any sporting event to see the manifestation of passion. People become fans of a sport or a team and are, by definition, fanatic about it. They extend their support and remain dedicated fans. Like purpose-driven loyalty, this is a unilateral relationship: the individual is a big fan of the sports team, but the sports team members don't even know the existence of this fan, which doesn't bother the fan in the least. Fans proudly wear their team colors and logos. They derive great pride and some identity from such a display.

3. Relationship-Driven. In relationships, both parties commit to each other, explicitly and implicitly. It is not only a commitment but a mutual expectation for most parts. While the first two tiers are relatively lifelong affiliations, relationships can be fluid and vary greatly in intensity.

4. Commerce-Driven. This is the lowest tier; it is the most transactional. Here there is a value exchange. The consumer pays for something or does something and gets something in return. As long as consumers see appeal or fairness in the value exchange, they will continue to engage with the brand. But they are very open to other possibilities and are quite easily tempted to stray. Companies offer incentives and rewards to try to get consumers to stick with them, mistakenly believing that they are engendering loyalty!

LONG LIVE AFFINITY!

In the Fifth Paradigm, marketers need to evolve their traditional long-term loyalty programs into effective "affinity platforms." *Affinity* is defined as "an attractive force between substances or particles that causes them to enter into and remain in chemical combination." No coincidences here. That definition is very close to the definition of quantum chemistry. We will be focusing on creating brand chemistry in the Fifth Paradigm. This perfectly describes what brands should strive to build—an affinity, a chemistry that keeps brands and consumers together, moment to moment. The moment that chemistry wanes, much like in a marriage, the twain will drift apart, except faster.

HOW TO BUILD BRAND AFFINITY AND CHEMISTRY

Work the entire loyalty hierarchy.

Leverage the four tiers of the hierarchy (purpose, passion, relationships, and commerce) by blending elements of each into the marketing strategy/mix. This means understanding consumers' mind-sets, at as granular a level as possible, in terms of what causes they care about (purpose), what they are fans of (passion), what their family or social networks are (relationship), and what their buying behavior is (commerce). All four should be incorporated simultaneously.

1. **Purpose.** If a given consumer is passionate about saving the environment, incorporate environment into the mix. Marketers may want to offer environmentally friendly products and packaging or may offer to contribute a small percentage of the profits for environmental protection, give a discount if they turn in their product packaging for recycling, and so on.

2. **Passion.** If the consumer is passionate about golf, at a minimum give golf-related imagery in the communication materials, and use golf media channels to communicate the message. In this example, marketers may need to construct benefits around golf, even if golf

is not connected with their category: maybe access to golfing events, professional golfers, or signed memorabilia.

3. Relationships. Family structure (single or a family person, with children or empty nesters), social network (people tend to flock to others with shared interests; marketers also get an idea of who their consumers are influenced by or whom they can influence), propensity to switch (let's call it a brand infidelity score)—these will be invaluable as marketers think about the product construct, offer construct, communication form, and content and media channels.

4. Commerce. Consumers want to know that they're getting a good value. Many even need to feel like they're getting a bargain to make a switch or persist with their current brand. Each consumer displays some price elasticity, a willingness to buy a product regardless of price, up to a point. But different price points affect consumer demand and choice. Marketers need to factor these in as they set their pricing and promotion strategies, to make sure they win consumers' preference every time.

Develop contextual preference management (CPM) platforms.

CPM allows marketers to work all tiers into a coherent plan relevant and valuable to both the consumer and the marketer.

Access real-time information about the consumer, whether purchase data or location.

This determines the next best offer or communication, when to make it, and in exactly which location.

Don't take contextual communication lightly.

Build consumer engagement before, during, and after the purchase. This point is sort of real-time CRM on steroids, to put it simplistically. Knowing what's happening with the consumer and what is happening around the consumer are both critical.

The key is to realize that consumer's preference has to be won every time—it is not one and done. And that ability to win every consumer transaction makes it necessary for the marketer to know what the context for each of those transactions is—the location, the occasion, the motivation—all at that very moment of truth. The objective is to appeal, convince, convert, satisfy, and repeat.

Leverage the traditional loyalty platforms.

Doing this, marketers continually develop a positive predisposition in consumers' minds. These loyalty platforms give the consumer a tangible anchor of reason and emotion to continue with a brand. Irrespective of how much they use it, consumers love the fact that they have an attractive option. It is like having an insurance policy. A consumer may or may not use it, but has the reassurance and satisfaction of having it.

Delight the consumer.

Nothing works better at holding on to consumers than giving them an intuitive and a delightful experience throughout the purchase life cycle, from buying to using it to returning to buy again.

In Quantum Marketing, loyalty management needs to transform into perpetual preference management platforms, creating programs for positive predisposition, and providing consumer experiences that delight. These need to work in tandem to attract and retain consumers, as much as their mind-sets permit. All these need to be associated with the brand, which is when brand affinity is born and strengthened.

In a world where consumers are tweeting in and out of a brand, hoping that they will stick with our brand exclusively for years is unrealistic. All of this means marketers have to create systemic programs and platforms that blend the art and science of preference management via context, experience, and emotion (see Figure 8).

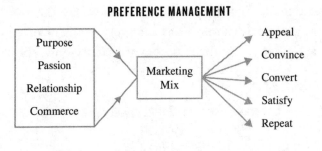

PREFERENCE MANAGEMENT

FIGURE 8

Give me affinity. Give me chemistry. Give me context. Give me relevance. Give me experience. And I will give you profitable growth and sustainable share gain. Those things can move a brand in the right direction in the quantum future.

TO SUMMARIZE . . .

➤ A majority of people seem not to exhibit loyalty in their marriage and personal relationships. So, marketers need to think about why, if at all, people will be loyal to their brands.

➤ Brands should recognize that consumers expect brands to be loyal to them, not the other way around.

➤ Marketers need to totally reimagine their loyalty strategies for the Fifth Paradigm.

➤ The loyalty continuum has four tiers of commitment. Marketers need to understand and assimilate all four into their affinity strategies.

➤ Marketers need to develop contextual preference management (CPM) platforms that allow them to work all tiers into a coherent plan that is relevant and valuable to both the consumer and the marketer.

CHAPTER 11

Advertising
(As We Know It)
Is Dead!

Something profound is happening in people's lifestyles. Everyone has a multiplicity of screens they are continually immersed in—tablets, smartphones, e-readers, and, of course, the trusty old TV or movie screen. And they are watching videos, chatting, reading, emailing, playing games, learning new things . . . In all, content comes gushing at them in a torrent, which includes an extraordinary amount of commercial messages. With this information bombardment, on all the screens, a constant stream of distractions vies for their attention, resulting in a tremendous fragmentation of focus. This is changing the physiology of the human brain and is reducing people's attention span. Today, it is estimated that the average human's attention span is slightly less than that of a goldfish, at under eight seconds![1]

A person is exposed, on average, to anywhere between three and five thousand commercial messages, every day.[2] Every single day!

This is an astronomical information overload and is humanly impossible to process.

So, a marketer needs to compete for the consumers' attention against anywhere between three and five thousand other messages every day, trying to cut through the clutter, inform them about their brand, product, or service, and inspire them to feel favorably and decide in their brand's favor.

What a huge challenge!

Now let's add a few more complications.

People want smooth, seamless, and uninterrupted experiences in their day-to-day lives. They do not like friction. They do not want interruptions. They are watching a nice movie, a serial drama, a news program, or a cat video, and then some stupid ad rudely intrudes into their vicarious world. People hate these intrusions. They seem to put up with these ads, because they are seeking free information, free entertainment, or some other free content. But there is nothing free in this world. People trade their attention for the entertainment or information they want. In other words, their attention is the currency.

How do consumers deal with this annoyance? They largely use ad time for going to the bathroom, or turning attention to their emails or whatever else may distract them.

People are getting smarter, as they should. They have discovered ad blockers. When activated, ad blockers prevent ads from appearing on their screens. Put another way, marketers have totally lost those consumers, been completely blocked, at least on that particular screen. These ad blockers are not rare or known only by the tech savvy. Today, the estimates for the number of consumers who use ad-blocking software range anywhere from six hundred million[3] up to two billion, *which is roughly a fourth of the world's population.*[4] And that number grows every year. These people are not accessible to marketers anymore, at least not through those screens on which they've installed these ad blockers.

Looking at consumer pain points, and in an effort to solve them effectively, some mobile phone manufacturers, particularly in Asia, are supporting ad blocker plugins on their browsers.[5] So, when a person buys a smartphone, she can turn the ad blockers on and shut the marketers out.

Now let's add yet another dimension: consumers wanting to move to a sane environment, free of all ads. So, instead of trading their attention, they are now trading their money, paying to get an ad-free experience. People subscribe to YouTube Premium for $12 per month, primarily to get an ad-free, smooth, and seamless video-viewing experience, both online and offline. Likewise, Hulu has a premium service without ads. They also have a significant scale.

Consumers are also going in droves to ad-free platforms such as Netflix, Amazon Prime, and a number of other smaller providers. To consumers, this is pure ad-free heaven! For me, it's freedom from the hell of being interrupted and bombarded by ads. In my own case, there have been any number of times when I'm watching a music video that an ad breaks right in the middle of the song! As a consumer, I hate it! Many times, I am so frustrated that either I turn away from the platform or look for a paid subscription option to get rid of the ads. As a normal human being, I welcome ad blockers and don't mind paying money to be in an ad-free environment to keep these pesky marketers away!

This is indeed a nightmare for all marketers. Marketers have to recognize that the traditional advertising model has to change because consumers are aggressively voting with their wallets, rushing into ad-free environments, and activating ad blockers at a humongous scale. How can we ignore this trend and hang on to the old, traditional ways of advertising?

Just to be provocative, to my team members, I keep saying that advertising is dead. Well, it's not entirely dead, but the way we know it today, it is certainly heading that way.

THE QUANTUM MARKETING SOLUTION

First and foremost, look at other ways of attracting and engaging consumers.

One very effective method is good old word of mouth. Marketers want people to talk about their brands and products. This is not new. Word-of-mouth publicity was considered to be one of the most reliable, dependable, credible, and effective ways to spread the message about a product, service, or brand. That fundamental principle still stands valid. In one way, it is almost "back to the future." Because people have other people in their physical and digital networks willing to hear from them, their communication doesn't get blocked. The idea is to make sure that people become spokespersons, ambassadors, promoters, or advocates of the brands, in a non-salesy fashion.

The key challenge is—how to do it economically and at scale?

Enter Quantum Experiential Marketing (QEM). Experiential marketing is in itself not new. It has been effectively done for decades. But what we are going to do in QEM is create and curate a combination of physical and digital experiences, coupled with a combination of traditional, digital, and social communication tactics. This could be a very powerful way of unlocking the potential of brand differentiation, consumer engagement, and preference management.

I term this transition from traditional advertising-led marketing strategies to experiential marketing strategies as: from storytelling to story making.

In this approach, first reach out to high-influence consumers, opinion leaders, or "prosumers" (a prospective consumer involved in or providing input into a product's design and development). Grab their attention and captivate their imagination with some unique experiences. These experiences should be flawless, leaving a lasting impression in their minds and hearts. When that happens, they have a very high propensity to tell the story of their experience to others. And weaved within that story is that the experience was enabled by a brand, in a subtle, credible, and appropriate way. Then, try to amplify that story.

The big question is, do people talk to their friends or relatives, to whomever is in their network, about brands? The answer is a big yes! Conversations, both positive and negative, around a brand don't happen only in the realm of commerce, but in people's day-to-day social streams. For example, research has shown that 92 percent of Instagram users follow a brand or something about brands.[6] In fact, brands can be made or destroyed overnight by one influential post!

Research has also shown that 74 percent of people make their brand choices and preferences based on the recommendation of people in their network, who have experience with a brand or with a product.[7] Word of mouth can also happen effectively outside of one's social network. Think of comments by other consumers on Amazon or Walmart.com, or ratings of drivers on Uber and Lyft. Deployed and managed effectively, QEM could be a very important channel for mobilizing preference and purchase of any given brand or product.

The key points to bear in mind are:

1. The experiences have to stand out, not necessarily in terms of luxury or high price, but in uniqueness and creativity. They need to be relevant and compelling to your consumers, and to the brand or category.

2. You should target these experiences to prosumers, influencers, and opinion leaders.

3. It's extremely critical that these consumers have a flawless, seamless, and extraordinary experience, to leave a lasting impression and long-term memory.

4. Throughout the experience, the brand association needs to be brought out in a natural, unforced manner. Consumers must be able to make a strong connection between their good experience and the

brand that enabled it. Experience, however great, without appropriate brand attribution, is pointless from the marketer's point of view.

5. Unobtrusively enable consumers to share their experiences, their stories, via their own communication channels. Bear in mind, if the experience is poor, they are going to talk about it even more aggressively. So, refer to point 3 above.

6. Amplify these stories, to ensure proper reach, through traditional, digital, and social channels.

7. Make sure that the experiences are scalable. One-and-done experiences, which few people can experience, are an interesting novelty. It is like creating an expensive piece of art that only a handful of people get to experience. And the daisy chain stops there. Pointless.

8. Make sure that the experiences offered are also economically viable and sustainable.

Points 3, 7, and 8 are the most difficult to accomplish, but they are the biggest factors in driving success or failure.

Airbnb, Lexus, the *Wall Street Journal,* and a number of companies have already started getting into the experiential space, quite effectively, creating and curating experiences that consumers truly care about.

Airbnb offered an experience in which consumers can go to the Louvre, after the museum closed to the public, and get an unhurried tour. They get to sit in front of Leonardo da Vinci's *Mona Lisa* and have a meal.[8] Literally, having a meal with the *Mona Lisa*! How cool is that! And at the end of the meal, they go to a specially prepared bed right within the glass pyramid in front of the museum building, where they can spend the night looking at the stars or sleeping in privacy. Overall, consumers come away feeling totally mind blown. Of course, their experience is all photographed to create a lasting record. And what do you think consumers do on their way back home or when they arrive? Can they wait to brag about it? Can they keep from posting their stories online? And should someone ask how they got their extraordinary experience, what would their answer be?

That's a terrific experience, very relevant for Airbnb. They are in the business of providing accommodations for travelers. So, they use fantastic experiences to grab consumers' attention and raise their opinion about the brand, which may give them significant salience in people's minds and robust differentiation from their competitors.

Another example is from Mastercard, where we made Priceless into an experiential platform, pivoting sharply from traditional advertising. Priceless, the advertising campaign, transformed into an experiential platform, which creates and curates experiences that money cannot buy—but available only through Mastercard. The campaign makes Priceless tangible. All the principles outlined above have been diligently implemented. Has it helped the company's brand and its business? You bet! The brand has grown from strength to strength, to being a top ten brand globally today, all the way from a position of number eighty-seven just a few years back.[9] Mastercard curates thousands of experiences around the world—it is an always-on experiential marketing engine!

Some brands can more easily visualize a direct link between the category they operate in and what looks like relevant experiences. Some may find it harder to do so. That is exactly where creativity comes in. And the brand that innovates and executes QEM flawlessly will find itself protected behind a "moat" of not-easily-duplicated advantages.

Shifting to another important part of the advertising world—the agencies. They are undergoing tectonic changes as we approach the Fifth Paradigm. Some companies are insourcing all or parts of agency activities. Consulting firms like Deloitte and Accenture got into what would be called the traditional agencies' domain. They are gobbling up stand-alone agencies to enhance their capabilities and are offering a full range of consulting-plus-agency services;

they are also adding fulfillment services. On the other side, ad agencies or agency holding companies are branching out beyond their traditional domain. For example, McCann bought Acxiom, the data powerhouse. As we look out toward the future, the definition of what an ad agency is and what services it will provide will be quite different from what it is today.

Coupled with this blurring of lines, some of the social media giants have started offering creative services to the marketers as a value add. And the gig economy is booming—freelancers and moonlighters are offering marketers high-quality creative services. And, of course, as we discussed in a previous chapter, the whole ecosystem is changing and is poised for a big transformation as AI-assisted creativity and new modes to showcase messages (VR, holographic projection, virtual trade shows, and such) continue to transform the processes. Agencies need to reinvent their models among all these shifting sands.

On another level, advertising value chains will be disrupted, with the elimination of many middlemen via blockchains. The economic returns on advertising dollars can actually go up, as a result.

Finally, in a world beyond cookies, the tracking, targeting, and retargeting of consumers is going to be totally altered. The emergence of digital IDs, the potential compensation of consumers from the ad revenues, will very likely happen.

The whole advertising ecosystem will be so different in the Fifth Paradigm that is not outlandish to say that advertising, as we know it today, is dying, if not dead.

TO SUMMARIZE . . .

➤ Consumer attention is scarce. And it is worsening by the day. Marketers need to think about how they engage consumers through alternative routes like Quantum Experiential Marketing.

➤ Data, AI, and other technologies will transform the world of advertising—from ad creation to new modalities of messaging to media optimization, everything will be recast dramatically.

➤ Marketers will succeed when they complement their creative side with tech savviness.

➤ Agencies will need to reinvent their models, even more dramatically.

➤ The ad value chain with its hordes of intermediaries will be disrupted by technologies like blockchains.

➤ A cookieless world is great for consumers' privacy protection. Marketers need to come up with alternative ways to effectively market.

CHAPTER 12

We Are Not Consumers, We Are People

Since the time formal and informal research started to inform advertising, marketers have been deeply focused on understanding consumers, their usage behaviors, attitudes, habits, and purchase history. Their main objective has always been to move consumers through the traditional purchase funnel effectively and quickly.

Marketers researched consumers with the goal of developing insights they could act on. They wanted to understand consumers deeply through their demographic, psychographic, and behavioral profiles. They could then group consumers into segments that could be targeted effectively. Marketers would study consumer needs, gaps in how those needs were being satisfied, pain points, and passion points. They would come up with products or solutions that would directly address those pain points and fill the gaps, thus satisfying the consumers' needs, both expressed and latent.

Marketers would model both purchase and usage behaviors. Some of the early purchase behavior models were like the AIDAS model: Awareness, Interest, Desire, Action, and Satisfaction.

According to this theory, a prospect was supposed to move through these different stages sequentially. First they become aware of the product or service, then they get interested in it, then they develop a desire to buy it. The goal is to get them to act upon that desire and purchase or consume the product. And once they experience the product or the service, they are satisfied, hopefully. This has been how consumers were studied, and their purchase behaviors were mapped out in excruciating detail.

Of course, since then, things have been turned upside down. Products and services have achieved a level of parity in terms of how they fulfill a need or eliminate a pain point. So, marketers started trying to delight the consumers as they use their products or services. But they typically designed the experience in the context of their product or category. That would be okay for BAU (Business as Usual) and if the product category and consumers remain static. However, there is a substantial crossover between different product categories. Under that pressure, the compartmentalized approach can be severely threatened.

Apple really gets it. It is one of the first major companies to have started a shift to human-centric experience, with their launch of the iPod at the beginning of this millennium. It allowed consumers to effortlessly access a thousand songs right from their pockets. Kudos to Apple; since then, they have created products so amazing that consumers did not even anticipate them, did not know they even needed them. But they've ended up being totally dependent on those devices. One of my favorite examples is the iPad. The user interface is so fantastic that even babies can use them intuitively. And senior citizens, who often struggle to learn new technologies, have been able to pick up and use an iPad without any trouble.

I still recollect such an interaction I had with my dad, when he was in his nineties. One day, he was staring at the DVD player's remote control, totally perplexed. Amused, I asked him what he was pondering on so intently. He said that the device had too many controls and he wasn't sure which one did what. I took a look at it. Turned out that I was no smarter. I had to fish out the user manual and read it patiently to learn how to fully work the damn remote control. Then, when I tried to teach my dad, it went right over his head. Compare that to a few years later when I gave him an iPad. It took him very little time or effort to begin using it quite happily. He was amazed that he could get any book from anywhere in the world onto his device and read it instantly. He was beyond delighted.

That, to me, is what CX and UX (user experience) should be like. What Apple did so extraordinarily well was to not merely fulfill the needs of consumers in a product category but to understand people in totality. This understanding resulted in their creating products that cut across product categories and made people's lives easy and delightful. That is a key approach in Quantum Marketing—you don't study consumers and their behavior, you study and understand people in totality. As Stan Sthanunathan, Executive Vice President of Insights at Unilever, said to me so aptly, "Product categories are a means to an end—the endgame is all about meeting the needs of people. For that, understanding peoples' holistic lives is what matters. If you want incremental improvements in your product, sure, go ahead and do all the consumer research you want. But if you are trying to break through, don't look at consumer research, do holistic people research. That's what will give you game-changing ideas and concepts!" More on this in a little while.

For any individual, consumption is but a sliver of their total life. Imagine the life of a person as a pizza. A small sliver pertains to the aspect of consumption. And the study of that consumption is essentially consumer research. But in reality, what happens outside that sliver affects consumption much more than what happens inside that sliver. Therefore, when marketers focus on optimizing consumer experience or consumer preference for their brands, they are focusing on the incremental and smaller opportunity of *consumer* behavior, as opposed to gaining substantial new ground by focusing on *human* behavior. Stan is absolutely spot on. We have to recognize that what happens in the totality of people's lives hugely affects their consumption behavior. The various aspects of people's lives are highly nested, highly interconnected, and highly interdependent.

Let's take the example of Dove Soap. This product had the unique differentiator of having one-fourth moisturizing cream in it. If Unilever stuck only to traditional consumer research, they would have been in an endless pursuit of ways to improve product superiority and communicating it in more convincing ways. These are not unimportant, and are indeed a key part of their BAU. However, when they looked at people's hopes, aspirations, and anxieties holistically, they found out that girls were under intense pressure to conform to unattainable stereotypical definitions of beauty, which was impacting their self-esteem and confidence. So, based on this insight, they elevated the brand by defining a higher order purpose for it—which is "all about real beauty, as opposed to stereotypes." Beauty is the authentic, unique, real, and best version of yourself. That platform took off and Dove has been enjoying growth, year after year, in an intensely competitive category, since.

Let's look at a different scenario. Suppose a company is looking at marketing a travel product. The normal tendency is to look at people's travel behavior and understand how, when, and why they travel. Marketers study how people research destinations, travel options, price comparisons, accommodations, and so on. Based on this, they see that consumers buy the offerings most appropriate to their travel needs, budgets, dates, and times, through a travel agent or directly with an airline. An inordinate amount of research goes into understanding these things. Is it relevant? Yes. Is it sufficient? Not at all. Let me explain.

In the past, parents of young children, say ten to twelve years old, would decide that they're going to take a vacation. They would plan to go to Disney World, and that they'd spend X number of days there in May when the schools were closed. They would do their research and go about making all the arrangements, booking the tickets, hotels, car rentals, and such. They would then inform the children, who in turn would be ecstatic.

Today, the reality has altered. First, children have become big participants in the decision-making process. Being digital natives and far smarter than their parents were at that age, they jump into the process by navigating the internet and watching videos. They are the R&D managers of the family, and they come up with options, comparisons, and preferences. Thus, they emerged to be key influencers on the family's decision-making process. The Quantum Marketer needs to understand family structures and their behavioral dynamics. Given the humongous amount of data available, they can gain incredible insights, that can guide their strategies in unconventional ways. Truthfulness, responsibility, and appropriateness are paramount here, as they navigate these emerging purchase dynamics.

In a person's life, there are different people, places, events, and acts that influence their consumption behavior. There are influencers, gatekeepers, financiers, and decision-makers around a person, be it within the family or in his/her broader network. The Quantum Marketer needs to understand all of these players and try to appropriately influence their preferences. This was not possible in the past, and isn't very much now, but it will be very doable and necessary for the imminent Fifth Paradigm. There will be a surfeit of data that people will have allowed us to use, and AI-powered analytics will provide insights through the entire marketing life cycle.

Back to the travel example. When marketers understand the totality of the individual's life, their overall campaign and communication approach might be less dependent on the destination or how to get there. The focus shifts from the product or service to making the experience of the individual or family better, not only on that imminent trip, but better in life overall.

Quantum Marketers look at the total life of their consumers and try to understand how they can add value. Once they take that approach and gain some insight, they then look at their product or service and assess whether they have the right offering or whether they need to create a new one or modify the existing one. They need to ask, "Do I have a product with which I can credibly, tangibly, and honestly address this person's situation and thereby create a business opportunity?" Then they can promote that product or service to them effectively in that life context.

People are flitting so much from brand to brand within a category, or even across categories, that traditional research probably offers very few valuable insights. Marketers are looking for answers in the wrong places. It's extremely important that the product play a role much larger than satisfying a person's need in a particular category. Actually, it needs to be plugged into the overall life of the individual. I might even dare to say that product marketing will become extinct in the next paradigm unless it is totally integrated into life marketing!

ANOTHER MAJOR SHIFT IN THE FIFTH PARADIGM

Historically, marketers would try to understand the purchase funnel and consumers' mind-sets before, during, and after a purchase. A huge shift is going to happen in the Fifth Paradigm. Marketers will do everything to make the purchase process disappear altogether. What does it mean? Let me explain.

Already, companies are trying to eliminate the need for a checkout line, as Amazon has done in their Amazon Go stores. A person can simply choose the items they want from the shelves, load up their shopping carts, and walk out. No need to stand in a checkout line to pay. A significant chunk of the purchase process has been eliminated. Kudos to them!

In online shopping, having a card on file has been a phenomenon for some time now. You enter your card credentials and shipping address once. And then, it is a single-click checkout thereafter. The checkout process has been shortened significantly.

Take another part of the purchase process that is getting turned upside down. In voice commerce, when you ask Alexa or Google

Home for some product information, what you get in return is either an explicit or implicit product or brand recommendation. And 70 percent or more of the people don't search any further.[1] They simply say, "Buy it." End of purchase! Here, these smart speakers are eliminating the need for people to go through the tedious process of searching, comparing, and making up their minds. It gets done for them, in nanoseconds. And the device learns the person's preferences with each interaction and comes up with even more compelling recommendations every subsequent time.

Here is another type of disruption: subscription services that send products. Subscribers don't need to remember or go through the whole process of reordering if their choice remains the same. This approach taps into their inertia, automates their choices, and forces their consumption. I was quite intrigued and impressed by Proctor & Gamble's recent launch of connected toothbrushes. Linked to a smartphone, these toothbrushes tell users how they are brushing their teeth, which parts are being left out, and so on. Based on users' brushing habits, how improbable is it for P&G to program the connected toothbrush to reorder the toothpaste, floss, or mouthwash as needed? It isn't science fiction—it is likely to happen.

Yet another mega disruption in the purchase funnel is automatic ordering via connected appliances. For example, Samsung has launched a smart refrigerator that knows what and how much the owners consume, and it reorders those items for them from the grocery store, thus unburdening them of this low-level tedium.

With the purchase process and funnel getting so disrupted, Quantum Marketers have to figure out how they will deal with consumer situations in the context of their life situations. Here are some critical components of their strategy:

➤ **Instant brand reassurance and instant brand motivation.** These will be ever more crucial in these automated purchase processes. The role of brand building, brand reputation, brand relevance, brand image and equity, and brand differentiation is mighty critical. This is actually going back to the basics.

➤ **Understanding the purchase channel dynamics.** Leverage them smartly, as opposed to letting them marginalize the brands. This needs deep knowledge in emerging digital technologies (like the Internet of Things and smart speakers), algorithms behind the recommendation engines of these various devices or platforms, preference drivers, real-time offer optimization methodologies via AI, and so on. These will be the new drivers for performance marketing.

➤ **Understanding a brand's potential moats.** We need these to stay relevant and competitively advantaged. These would be less about the products themselves but more about the surrounding systems, packaging, Intellectual Property, emotional hooks, and so on.

One of the big things various innovators are trying to do is to make the entire purchase process automated and free consumers from the burden of having to think about a product, learn about it, make a choice, and buy it. In some sense, people are being cut out of the purchase process! The algorithm or the machine takes the burden away from the individual and completes the purchase. How exciting!

Marketers absolutely need to study and understand how people buy and consume products and services. But that will not be adequate for the future. Everything around and about people is changing, and those changes are going to drive their consumption behavior, process, and pattern. Many categories of products will get eliminated or altered, based on the tectonic changes happening all around. So, it is critical that marketers don't anchor their marketing strategies, from insights all the way through the entire life cycle, solely on consumer studies. Studying people holistically, and marketing to them as people and not as consumers, is the Quantum Marketing way.

TO SUMMARIZE . . .

➤ For any individual, consumption is but a sliver of their total life. When marketers focus on optimizing consumer experience or consumer preference, they are focusing on the incremental and smaller opportunity of *consumer* behavior, as opposed to gaining substantial new ground by focusing on *human* behavior.

➤ A Quantum Marketer looks at the total life of their consumer and tries to understand how they can add value, unconfined by their existing product category. And then they create and promote that product, service, or bundle to them effectively in the right context of their life.

➤ Among many other disruptions, the purchase process and purchase funnel will be completely disrupted in the Fifth Paradigm.

➤ Many mundane activities, which include making routine purchases, will be on autopilot, such that people aren't as involved in making those purchase decisions. Marketers need to understand the implications and figure out their models in such an environment.

CHAPTER 13

Marketing to Businesses and Machines

The entire field of business-to-business marketing is several generations behind when it comes to tapping into emotions, incentives, aesthetics, and softer aspects of marketing. On some of the processes and ROI measures, however, the field has gone past consumer marketing in a big way. Business-to-business marketing has typically focused on technical communication with lesser reliance on, if any, human sensibilities. The reliance is on data and performance claims within communication elements, which by nature tend to be less interesting and hardly inspiring.

The fundamental premise of B2B marketing is that business decisions are based on technical specifications, logical processes, economics, and performance guarantees. Somehow, the universal perception, and very wrongly so, is that emotions play very little role in this space, and they are often viewed with some level of disdain.

As much as economics play a key role, behavioral economics also play a huge role here. And System 1 thinking (see chapter 8—"The

Sciences behind Marketing") doesn't restrict itself when a person is in a work situation. System 1 is System 1, irrespective of where the person is and what he/she is doing. It is critical that B2B marketers appeal to System 1, to gain success.

What most marketers miss is the blindingly obvious fact staring at us—businesses don't run by themselves, they are run by very real people. These people, even in a business context, behave like human beings, just as they do when they are outside the business setting. When marketing to a person, marketers study that person's psychology—aspirations, fears, insecurities, pain points, and so on. Why, when talking about a business product, would they then suddenly switch to communicating with that person in a "business-like" tone? I call this the Dr. Jekyll–Mr. Hyde syndrome of marketing. When trying to market a soap or a vacation, marketers talk to consumers in a particular way, appealing to all of their faculties. But they turn cold and start talking only to the rational side of their brain when marketing a business product to them. Marketers assume a level of formality and focus on things that are boring and uninteresting and uninspiring. That's a big, fallacious approach of many B2B marketers.

We need to recognize that people are the ones who run businesses, at least for now. And when these people make purchase decisions, though we may think they base their decisions purely on rationale or logic, their decision-making dynamic is exactly the same when they make decisions in their personal lives.

Of course, there are different levels of analyses that go into the decision-making process in both contexts. In B2B, decision-makers are not bearing the economic burden of the decision directly; they have teams helping them evaluate the facts more thoroughly, and there are parameters set up by their respective companies for evaluating any product or service (three quotes to be obtained, for example). All these speak to the inputs and the context. The eventual decision is reached in exactly the same manner as in their personal lives—it is influenced by their emotions, feelings, and gut. As much as marketers would like to think otherwise, that is the fact and the reality. B2B marketers must realize that emotion has a clear and a significant role in the decision-making process.

B2B marketing targets can be thought of in five very broad categories: large businesses, governments, not-for-profit organizations, small and medium businesses, and start-ups. They each have different behavioral characteristics along a continuum of the interplay between rules-based decision-making and the emotion involved (see Figure 9).

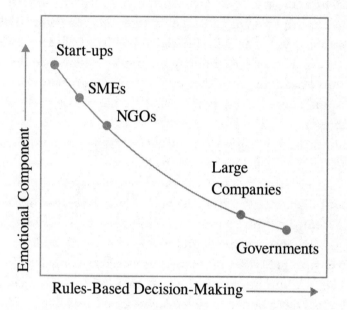

FIGURE 9

Each of these categories needs to be marketed to differently, because rules and emotions in each category operate at varying levels to influence the decision-making.

Whether it is B2B marketing or consumer marketing, at the end of the day, it all should be about P2P marketing: person-to-person. People-to-people, human-to-human marketing. In Quantum Marketing, that's what marketers do. They humanize businesses, because human beings run the businesses. They market to those human beings, in a human fashion, who are making decisions for their businesses.

Historically, when marketers would try to market a product or a service to other companies, they had to behave like it was one company marketing to another company.

B2B communication needs to be authentic, not formal. B2B marketers need to go out of their way to humanize the entire presentation. The approach, style, and sensibilities of B2B marketing will converge with those of consumer marketing. They will all be P2P marketing. Says Diana O'Brien, Global CMO of Deloitte, "B2B marketers have an unprecedented opportunity to humanize their relationship by tapping into the innate passions of their clients and leveraging new business models that support more participation, collaboration, and co-creation with them."

Currently, campaigns to create awareness and generate leads for businesses are typically done via trade channels—be it trade sites or publications, conferences, trade shows, venue-based billboards (like airport billboards, which are very effectively leveraged by Deloitte and Accenture), white papers and other content publishing, advertising on business channels, and so on.

In Quantum Marketing, marketers would not only humanize all this content, without losing the facts their prospects are searching for, but overlay a bunch of rich insights from areas like psychology, neurology, behavioral economics, and sensory sciences. For example, for a business product, they would do as rigorous a design of UX as they would for a consumer product. They would create the ads as interesting and enthralling as possible, not only highlighting the benefit of the product but also appealing to the emotional side of the folks involved in decision-making. They would deploy influencer marketing, just as they would with consumer products. They would deploy Multisensory Marketing, just as . . . You get the drift.

Customer relationship marketing is well developed in the Fourth Paradigm. In the Fifth Paradigm, this will go to the next level, integrating with real-time data from across business and consumer spheres, leveraging location-based targeting, and personalizing communication. CRM will integrate contextual preference management platforms in a very native and compelling manner.

Technology will play a huge transformational role too. For example, COVID-19 taught us that we need to and can work remotely. And it wasn't all that bad. Virtual meetings—one to one, one to many, and many to many—have all been tested and are quite functional. This technology will only keep advancing, given the humongous boost to productivity and cost efficiency that remote video conferencing can bring about. Now that we've tasted that, we need to ask ourselves how we can port these capabilities to B2B marketing. For example, can our seminars and conferences be not only virtual but immersive via VR? Can we have VR trade shows? Can we have VR-based, interactive virtual product demos that also leverage augmented reality? With 5G coming down the pike and the continuing advances in various related areas, this is not only going to be real but will soon become the norm.

AI has already influenced B2B marketing in a big way. For example, a lot of companies are already doing their Request for Proposal (RFP) responses using AI. The AI engine looks at the RFP, understands the questions being asked, looks into internal databases, including how the company responded to other RFPs in the past. Based on this, it comes up with compelling responses, which are as good as or better than those done by an army of staff. It does this in a fraction of the time, more accurately, and with more up-to-date information.

Drone delivery, 3-D printing, and other technologies are going to be game changing. They cut down timelines on the one hand, reduce inventory on the other, and can materially affect customers' businesses.

Game playing is seen by most people to be purely in the purview of kids and nerds. Surprisingly, it is restricted to neither. Gamification, using elements of game playing in other areas, is applicable to every person, irrespective of how mature and elevated they think they are. Gamification is applicable in the B2B space too. I have seen some brilliant prototypes across multiple B2B situations. For example, I saw a demo where a gaming app shows a hospital CEO, in a fun way, how to allocate resources. In reality, the game is drawing the attention of the CEO to some of the more obscure product areas the marketer is trying to sell, demonstrating their value subtly but unmistakably. We are just beginning to see this area developing, and deployment cannot be that far out. Whether this will be a dominant way to engage customers is still to be proven. But it is hard to ignore that every person has an inner child, an instinct to play, and an inclination to have fun. Gamification taps into that exact mindset to communicate, engage, and deliver marketing objectives in an unconventional manner.

MARKETING TO MACHINES

In the Fourth Paradigm, we learned how to market to machines. When a machine (actually, the algorithm behind it) decides which brand will show up and where it ranks in an online search, it is important to first market to the machine, which then puts our brand in front of consumers. Marketers had to learn how to influence that machine, that is, how to position the brand best in the eyes (logic) of that algorithm. I am talking about search engine optimization (SEO) and search engine marketing (SEM).

Now, thanks to AI, the machines are getting more sophisticated, and marketers need to figure out how to market to them. In a literal sense, it is a set of machines on your side marketing to a set of machines on the other side. This is an important part of the marketing process, and it can break all the other efforts if not done right.

In other words, marketers need to gear up to the new realities and rethink their machine-marketing strategies, algorithms, and content. For example, when a consumer asks Alexa for a product, Alexa serves the brand based on some logic someone programmed it with. Unless marketers know how to show up the right way,

Alexa may not even mention their brand and it will never enter the consumer's purchase consideration. That is a death knell. As mentioned in a previous chapter, smart speakers are proliferating; people are using them in large numbers to make their purchases. Seventy percent of the time, they rely on what Alexa recommends. So marketers just cannot ignore this very important new medium for marketing. Another interesting dimension will be how these smart speakers and assistants transition into a business-to-business context.

All this gets amplified with the advent of the Internet of Things, like smart refrigerators, all of which can potentially influence brand choice when the purchase has to be made. To be effective, marketers need to figure out how to market to these machines.

TO SUMMARIZE . . .

➤ Marketing to businesses is still not as evolved as it is to consumers. Marketers need to realize that businesses are run by people, who are emotional beings and make decisions for themselves or their companies with a healthy dose of emotion.

➤ Consumer relationship marketing will go to the next level, leveraging insights and technologies from the consumer marketing world.

➤ New technologies will advance marketing to businesses dramatically—virtual conferences, virtual trade shows, immersive VR-AR product demos, gamification, and so on are all going to open new dimensions and possibilities, new cost efficiencies, and new layers of effectiveness.

➤ Marketers need to determine how they will market to the new intermediaries in the purchase process—machines and their algorithms. Smart speakers and the Internet of Things will accentuate this need.

➤ Marketers need to build knowledge, capabilities, and processes to adapt to this new environment in the Fifth Paradigm and have your own Quantum Marketing playbook to win.

CHAPTER 14

Power in Partnerships

With complexities and dynamics swirling around in the Fifth Paradigm, most marketing initiatives will involve tapping into and pulling together inputs from multiple sources and executing through multiple resources, and assets from yet another set of resources. Marketers cannot do all of this by themselves. They need partnerships, across every aspect and stage of marketing.

INTERNAL PARTNERSHIPS

Clearly, marketing cannot be an island in an organization. CMOs need to move the marketing function into the mainstream of their companies, focusing on moving the brand, business, and competitive edge forward. This requires them to build strong bridges with every other function and department in the company. While this might seem like a blindingly obvious statement that is equally applicable to every function, it actually is quite different for marketing. Unlike a function like finance, legal, or IT, which typically the

CEO and the other C-suite executives understand, marketing is less understood. This may not be true for CPG companies, but it is quite true with most other sectors, as discussed before. Hence, there is that extra mile and more that the stewards of marketing need to go, to mainstream the function, build solid internal partnerships across the board—from finance to legal to IT to HR. In smaller companies, this could be easier to achieve as there are fewer people, each of whom will be wearing multiple hats. Regardless, internal partnerships are vital for the success, and they can make or break the function. Let's look at each partnership area.

Information Technology

Not only is technology a key enabler and driver of sound marketing, but there is an increasing level of confluence between marketing abilities and technology capabilities. Given this, it is imperative to have a very close and strong partnership with the CIO. Without this critical partnership, the marketing function is going to miss the boat. I would daresay that this is probably the most important internal partnership, other than with your CEO, in determining the marketing function's operational success.

CFO

At this time, there is no real excuse for not getting more robust ROI measurements from marketing. Metrics and measures should be in place and be robust enough to give CFOs what they're looking for. Even better, marketing should have its own CFO who also reports into the company CFO. CFOs, on behalf of the company, would legitimately ask tough questions regarding every sizeable investment, and marketing dollars are typically sizeable. So, it is critical for the CFO and CMO to have a strong partnership, be on the same page, and navigate the ups and downs of business cycles together.

Human Resources

As the field of marketing is transforming, talent management within the marketing function is going to be extremely important. A strong relationship with the CHRO or chief people officer is a must. Given that the skills and capabilities that Quantum Marketing needs are way different than they have been up until now, talent acquisition and development will be critical. CMOs need to ensure that their team is well equipped, well trained, well graded, well compensated, and well rewarded. When it comes to, say, job rotations of the team members, particularly outside marketing, the partnership between HR and marketing will be invaluable. HR needs to be in sync with the marketing vision, strategy, and agenda.

Legal

Another key internal partnership is with the company's general counsel or Chief Legal Officer. With significant consumer protections and regulations cropping up in an unprecedented fashion, marketers need to not only understand what the regulatory landscape looks like but also what the boundaries and opportunities are. They also need a close partnership with their policy and regulatory colleagues to make sure that they will guide and help influence the formulation of upcoming marketing regulations in a way that is fair to the consumers but also pragmatic for the marketers to operate within, both in spirit and word.

CEO

Finally, marketers need to have a very good partnership with their CEO. That's very important to make sure that they are driving the marketing vision and agenda totally in line with and supporting the CEO's vision for the company as a whole. It's important that there is buy-in from the top of the house, or else the marketing agenda can fall apart. Since many C-suite members lack an understanding of what marketing does or can do, and the value it brings or can bring, it is even more critical that the CEO is committed to the marketing function. If the CEO is not a believer in marketing, it will be a huge challenge for the marketer. The marketer needs to invest time and effort to bring the CEO up the marketing curve, show the promise inherent in the function, and give proof to show its impact. The marketer needs to demonstrate the value of the function to prevent it from being marginalized. If, after all that, things don't change, it is better for marketers to evaluate whether they want to spend the rest of their career fighting furiously, internally and externally, to do the right thing for the company. Or simply move.

Stakeholders

Depending on the structure of a company's overall organization structure, marketing also needs to have partnerships with areas such as product management (if it is not within marketing), public relations (if it is still a stand-alone function), sales, and customer service. Consumer engagement with the company or brand doesn't begin and end with marketing. There are other stakeholders who enable or deliver different aspects of the consumer experience and brand perception. Marketing needs to be connected very deeply to them and to ensure that the insights that are generated within the function are distributed throughout every aspect of the organization. Every consumer touch point with the company is an opportunity to enhance and reinforce the brand promise and experience. And everyone who touches consumers, customers, or prospects is a brand ambassador. Marketers are brand stewards, not brand owners. If marketers adopt that mind-set, they will be able to get the entire company to rally behind the brand, as they should. After all, the brand belongs to everyone in the company.

AGENCY PARTNERSHIPS

The ad agency will continue to play a key role, irrespective of everything else that will be transforming around us. As much as data and technology will be critical for effective and impactful communication, creativity will be a huge differentiator. It will enable connections with the hearts and souls of the people—customers, consumers, and prospects. Very few companies will have the wherewithal to build in-house capabilities at scale and with top-notch talent. For the rest of us, we need agency partnerships. This includes research agencies, media agencies, and PR agencies, though I will emphasize creative agencies here. Ad agency partners are the biggest asset to the marketers. They need to understand completely what the vision is, what the strategy is, what the priorities are, and what constraints exist. When they get all that, they can support marketers in the most appropriate way. Marketers need to have the right agency with the right attitude with a very creative team that is completely in sync with them and in step through the entire journey to success.

The partnership should be such that the agency is respected and that their people are treated as equals and held accountable. The agency's operations should be transparent as well. Unfortunately, many marketers view agency partners as vendors, those who produce work only on a project-by-project basis. The agency is not clued into the overarching vision and strategy, so they cannot give their best effort. As unpopular as it may seem in an environment of relentless cost cutting, there has to be a long-term commitment to agency partners. We have to invest in the kind of partnership that marketers want to build with them. Agency partners need to not only understand the business but understand the soul of the brand. This doesn't happen just by reading some brand-positioning statements. Understanding the soul of the brand is very experiential, it is evolutionary, and it is very deep. I'd also caution marketers to not make agency selection and maintenance primarily a procurement exercise. Procurement and vendor sourcing have very important supporting roles to play in getting the best contract terms. I would be concerned if procurement teams, rather than the marketing team, drives agency selection, which is a crucial step toward creative excellence.

INNOVATION PARTNERSHIPS

Innovation, alongside creativity, is always going to lead to a significant competitive advantage. I don't preclude partnerships with large companies, but I find partnerships for innovation are most effective with start-ups or companies scaling up. They are innovative and impressive, hungry for growth, and very agile. It's important to form strong partnerships with such companies to take your brand's promise and delivery to the next level. In my career, I found that most of the best ideas come from these kinds of small companies with brilliant founders. These partnerships tend to be highly symbiotic, where the marketers get access to the right ideas and intellectual property while being able to provide a phenomenal platform for these start-ups. We grow together.

And marketers need to manage innovation partnerships to make sure intellectual capital and best practices are retained. Partnerships should provide some kind of a competitive advantage even after the exclusivity periods end.

TECHNOLOGY PARTNERSHIPS

To effectively leverage the power of technology, marketers need to either have their own powerful toolbox and resources or have effective partnerships with tech vendors. Given the rate of change, it might be prudent for companies to not get stuck with legacy systems but be able to effectively cobble together versatile and modular solutions via tech companies that develop, maintain, and update their platforms. Given that most marketers are not deeply knowledgeable about technology, they need to get their CIO or external partners to create the solution that is right for them. Modularity, versatility, interoperability, scalability, and security are but some of the key parameters with which to gauge and evaluate the various tech solutions. Also, to remain nimble, the tech interface should be simple. Marketers should be able to use it themselves without putting in requests to IT or the vendor all the time.

MEDIA AND PASSION PARTNERSHIPS

Traditionally, media has been a core area of marketing. The media industry is going to get further disrupted; therefore, they will be looking for medium- to long-term partnerships, new business models, and new pricing structures. For companies that spend significantly in media, it is critical that their marketing folks stay very close to the developments in this space, identify opportunities for partnerships beyond the traditional exchange of money for space, and try to understand the implications of what is coming down the pike to their own marketing and media strategy.

I call partnerships with sports, music, dining, and so forth passion partnerships. Good quality assets in these key passions are in very short supply, which leads to the rising prices. On the other hand, new categories like eSports and holographic tours will divert some consumer attention and, therefore, marketing funds. When cutting through the clutter is already proving to be a challenge, sponsorships can play a vital role in both gaining consumer attention as well as enabling experiential marketing.

PUBLIC-PRIVATE PARTNERSHIPS (PPP)

There are many areas that, historically, have been the sole domain of governments. When it comes to areas like smart cities, health care, and community education, governments cannot do everything by themselves. That's where public-private partnerships play a big role in bringing about transformation within communities. These partnerships don't have to be charitable or not-for-profit initiatives. They can be for profit, and companies can build models that will give an appropriate return to their investments, even as the initiatives help improve communities. Typically, PPPs unite a government entity, a nongovernment organization, and a private or publicly traded company.

I don't need to look much further than Mastercard for excellent examples. One is City Possible, which helps address the challenges large cities around the world have with population growth. For example, in partnership with Cubic, we researched and installed an entire new mobile payment system for the London Underground. The benefit for Londoners was that the endless queues to access the underground have been shortened. And the arrangement also benefits Mastercard. It is a win-win all around.

INDUSTRY AND TRADE PARTNERSHIPS

Partnerships with industry and trade bodies can be very beneficial, not only to a company but, as the name suggests, to the entire industry. Time and again, industry bodies take up the agenda that is important to its members or partners and navigate policy making, standard setting, educating stakeholders, and so on, which no single company can do on its own. As self-evident as the opportunities might seem, it is surprising how little marketers are involved in the affairs of industry.

When so much change is happening all around us, it is important to have some standards for interoperability for everyone's benefit. If each new innovation or development in an industry comes with its own standards, inconsistent and incompatible with other parts of the ecosystem, it will be a complete mess.

For example, look at the various social media platforms. Each has its own standards. There's no interoperability across other platforms. Marketers, therefore, cannot measure return on investment across these platforms in a cohesive fashion, for optimizing their investments in future campaigns. So, under the auspices of World Federation of Advertisers and in collaboration with the Association of National Advertisers, a number of agency holding companies, the main social media platforms, and a large number of brands formed an initiative called GARM (Global Alliance for Responsible Media) to address these anomalies. Marketers should actively devote a small but focused portion of their time to these kinds of industry affairs and partnerships.

LOCAL COMMUNITY PARTNERSHIPS

Our world is getting truly globalized and will continue to be so into the next paradigm. Local communities, however, are becoming an increasingly important focus for consumers—eat local, buy locally made, vibrant localities, local support groups. Establishing partnerships with local communities to genuinely make a difference, with brand and product affiliations transparently displayed, will be a significant trend: the macrocosm and microcosm dancing in harmony. Brands first to the communities will always be the first love of the people in those communities and will enjoy a more positive predisposition. The COVID-19 pandemic has shown the power of these efforts. Look at examples like Instagram's Live Donations feature, which took advantage of a 70 percent spike in the brand's traffic to help communities affected by the virus.[1] A number of research studies on this subject make for interesting reading but, more importantly, are instructive for future marketing strategies.

PART-TIME, CONTRACT, AND FREELANCE WORKERS

Another important area rapidly evolving is the contract- or freelance-worker economy. Normally, when companies hire people, they assume that the bulk of them will work with them for a number of years. The company gives them training and long-term incentives and hopes to retain the best talent. But with the pace of change, and with the new generation's strong bias toward freelance work, it's extremely important that marketers take note and see how the new way of working will be different in the future. How will the marketing function's structure accommodate freelance workers? How would the processes work with freelancers, seamlessly? How can roles be split between multiple part-time employees? How will the confidentiality of work be preserved? In hotels, front office staff do shifts. Is there any opportunity or advantage in having marketers work on a given project in shifts? How can the creative and executional excellence be ensured? Part-time or freelance workers are here to stay. Marketers need to rethink their people and organizational models in this context and make the best out of it.

TO SUMMARIZE . . .

Marketing is not going to be the same in the Fifth Paradigm. There will be new capabilities, new infrastructure, new opportunities, powerful technologies. There will be rich and overwhelming data availability, ability and an opportunity to do real-time marketing in the truest sense of the term, and there will be measurement methodologies that give precise ROIs. The work cultures are going to be different and partnerships will become a key ingredient to progress and success. New and substantial risks will be there that need to be accounted for. All these will necessitate a rethink of how the marketing function is going to work tomorrow. Marketers need to put a well-orchestrated machinery in place that works smoothly and brilliantly and brings Quantum Marketing together like magic. And partnerships will be vital to powering this.

CHAPTER 15

Purpose as an Imperative

Purpose driven. It's the catchphrase for life coaches, TV ministers, and corporate advisers. It's the in thing within corporate circles and the media. The basic idea: companies have to not only do good for their shareholders and employees but also do good for society at large. Unfortunately, a level of political correctness clouds out serious examination of purpose and whether "purpose driven" truly drives better company performance.

A number of studies tried to demonstrate that organizations that have an explicit purpose, which are purpose driven, fare better than those companies that do not. One study says purpose-driven companies outperform the market by 42 percent.[1] I have personally gone through some of these studies. The direction seems to be right, though the causal links (one thing causing another), as opposed to correlations (two things happening together, but one not causing the other), are less evident in a definitive manner. And one cannot definitively say that companies without an explicit purpose don't do as well.

Purpose is seen as something every company should have and write in its annual report. As Kellogg School professor Robert

Quinn wrote in *Harvard Business Review* in 2018, "When a company announces its purpose and values, but the words don't govern the behavior of senior leadership, they ring hollow. Everyone recognizes the hypocrisy, and employees become more cynical. The process does harm."[2] Journalists are rightly asking the tough questions about this lack of authenticity, this "purpose washing," and they are challenging the very hypothesis. We have a collective responsibility to find the truth.

Different companies focus on different areas, environmental protection and sustainability, animal welfare, diversity and inclusion, fighting hunger and poverty, gender balance, and so on. But many get confused between what a purpose is and what cause marketing is. Many see these two as interchangeable, when in reality they are two different things. Let's start with the definition of purpose and distinguish it from a cause, what most marketers center activities on.

Purpose is the fundamental reason why a company exists. It is a North Star, a guiding principle, a core value of a company. We're not talking about the company being principled—that's a different thing altogether. The company exists for reasons beyond maximizing shareholder returns, maximizing employee satisfaction, and satisfying customers, which are business-as-usual (BAU) goals.

On the other hand, *cause* marketing is more about a specific set of initiatives, campaigns, or activities that do good for the society. A company can execute a series of causes without having a single-minded purpose, other than a broad philosophy that it wants to do good.

Purpose is a North Star and cause marketing is the road map. The two should be tied. Purpose is why a company exists and what is guiding it, whereas cause marketing is about specific initiatives that do good for the society.

When cause marketing is done solely by identifying causes that benefit society, without being tied together into the company's larger narrative or business mission, it will be nothing more than an isolated series of good activities lacking purpose. So, it is very important for marketers to identify those causes that emanate from, or drive toward, their company purpose.

Now, is purpose really necessary, or is it just political correctness? A brand doesn't pursue purpose solely to make the company do better or maximize shareholder value. A company should pursue purpose for two overarching reasons.

1. It is a philosophy. If marketers are in a position to do good for the society, why would they *not* do it? It's a fundamental value. Do they just want to be self-serving, or do they want to do something good for society at large, because it is important to do and they can do it?

2. It builds trust. Today, as we will discuss in the ethics chapter, there is a huge trust deficit that just gets worse every day. Customers perceive exploitation and deception all around. Companies that have a well-articulated purpose and back that purpose sincerely through appropriate cause-marketing initiatives; companies that tell their story honestly with an authentic message that is coherent, cogent, compelling, and convincing—these companies will stand out in the eyes of consumers.

When I look at the future, "purpose drivenness" is clearly going to be a huge differentiator for companies. In a world of real or perceived exploitation and deceit, consumers' perceptions of purpose-driven companies that seem to be genuinely doing good will be hugely positive.

There are different models companies use to pursue purpose. Many companies have a foundation. They put some money into the foundation, which keeps doing its good work. That's a good beginning, and by doing that, companies get some tax advantages too. Instead of paying taxes, they might as well put the money in a foundation and get some credit from society for the good they're doing for the community. This is one approach.

Then, there is the model of corporate social responsibility, or

CSR. CSR initiatives can be run by a foundation or as an adjunct to it. The approach here is that every corporation has a social responsibility and they need to deliver on it, measure it, and put it in their annual reports.

Typically, the funding for the above two is discretionary and ad hoc. In a good year, more money goes into the foundation or CSR initiatives. In other years, not so much. This can lead to an inconsistency of commitment.

For purpose-driven companies, building continuous momentum and maintaining consistency is the key. From a brand perspective, unless a purpose is consistently pursued or a cause is fought for, consumers will not associate the company with that cause or perceive them as a purpose-driven company. That's very important to remember.

Secondly, when foundation and CSR activities become some kind of a sideshow, only a small set of people are focused on them. The rest of the company is focused on business as usual. With only a small, limited part of that company focused on purpose and causes, and not the entire organization, companies are missing a huge opportunity.

Purpose is truly brought to life when it is completely blended into the core of the company's business model. Mastercard's purpose statement is: "Connecting Everyone to Priceless Possibilities." That philosophy is embedded into the organization, and the causes it supports are weaved into its marketing promotions and campaigns, into the core of its business. When that happens, the impact you make is at a very different level altogether. I'll give you a few examples.

Mastercard wanted to raise awareness of cancer and help find cures, so it started by striking a partnership with Stand Up To Cancer. We created a program in which each time a card member pays with a Mastercard at any restaurant during the promotional period, the company would contribute a small fraction of those proceeds to Stand Up To Cancer. They would then deploy that money to form what they call dream teams of extraordinary medical researchers from around the world, and these dream teams would come together and work on discovering cures for cancer. But what's beautiful about this model is that this becomes a very sustainable activity: each time it runs this promotion, Mastercard's share within the restaurant category goes up and the incremental revenues thus generated fund the drug discovery research. That makes this a sustainable model, by blending cause marketing into the core business activities, driven by a larger purpose.

Some other examples:

➤ Microsoft is doing a brilliant job creating accessibility tools for people with special needs. That is not just a charitable activity but actually a core part of their business and how they build their products. Special needs kids in the UK have designed gaming controllers. Workers with disabilities have designed gaming accessory packaging. And Microsoft technology has helped ALS patients speak through their eyes.

➤ SAP hires young adults with autism as coders. They realized that people with autism make very good coders, so they are changing their hiring processes to help these young adults transition into the work environment. The results are extraordinary. They have partnered with Integrate Employment Advisors to systematically add employees on the autism spectrum.

➤ Patagonia is another excellent example of a company integrating purpose with its business practices, totally. Their mission says: "Patagonia is in the business to save our home planet." The company donates 1 percent of their sales to grassroots environmental organizations. They spend a lot of time and effort advocating for environmental causes. They even have folks decked out for environmental activism.

There is another interesting angle to pursuing purpose called data philanthropy, where private companies contribute their proprietary data for public good. Such data could be used by NGOs, academia, or governments to identify, analyze, or resolve issues that affect communities. Here is an example: LinkedIn's open-source data project called the Economic Graph is a digital representation of the global economy based on more than six hundred million members, fifty thousand skills, twenty million companies, fifteen million open jobs, and sixty thousand schools. Through mapping every member, company, career, and school, it can spot trends like talent migration, hiring rates, and in-demand skills by region. These insights connect people to economic opportunity and give governments and NGOs a chance to better connect people to opportunities.[3] While LinkedIn has since closed the initiative, the purpose of providing this example is to demonstrate the concept and application of data philanthropy.

Eighty-three percent of people globally believe brands have the power to make the world a better place, and 87 percent say brands must stand up for what they believe in. Eighty-four percent believe businesses have a responsibility to spur social change, and 64 percent say they will buy or boycott a brand based on its stance on a social or political issue.[4]

Purpose drivenness connects cause marketing and business outcomes. Purpose is not fluffy, nor is it meant for political correctness or annual reports. Companies need to pursue purpose because it is the right thing to do, because consumers are willing to vote with their wallets in favor of purpose-led brands, because younger generations of people want to work only in purpose-driven organizations. They are even willing to take a cut to their compensation to work for a company they believe does good for the society and is purpose driven, so it's a huge competitive advantage to attract and retain top talent.[5]

TO SUMMARIZE . . .

➤ Commitment to purpose has to come from the top of the house, from the CEO. Marketers should help shape it, craft it, and give it a compelling narrative.

➤ Embed purpose into the core model of the business; don't make it into a sideshow.

➤ Identify a select set of cause-marketing initiatives that would dovetail into the company's purpose.

➤ Do not keep chasing the shiny pennies. Consistency is critical to making a real difference.

➤ Long-term commitment is very important.

➤ Marketers need to tell the company purpose story, authentically, and not in an advertising or sales mode. Otherwise, it will be seen as merely self-serving.

➤ Employees of the company need to embrace the company purpose and rally around the cause-marketing initiatives.

➤ Do not create a brand name for each of the cause-marketing initiatives. If you do, nothing will stick to the overall brand. It will only diffuse the brand impact and brand equity.

➤ Ensure that right partnerships are established. Get partners who have fantastic reputations and partner with them effectively and for the long term.

➤ Make sure that there is synergy between the foundation, the CSR initiatives, and the cause-marketing initiatives.

CHAPTER 16

Ethics and Brand Karma

Someone recently forwarded me a link to George Carlin's stand-up routine on advertising and marketing. He joked about the "tricks" marketers and advertisers have up their collective sleeves, literally dozens of them. "Whenever you're exposed to advertising in this country," he says, "you realize all over again that America's leading industry is still: the manufacture, distribution, packaging, and marketing of bullshit."

It is funny, but, sadly, it also reflects the public's perception of marketing as lacking conscience or ethics.

Ethical behavior is not only a fundamental requisite in any civilized society but should be the guiderail to any individual's daily life and to any marketer's professional life. Lack of ethical behavior can and should erode consumer trust. It is shocking that only 34 percent of consumers trust the brands they buy.[1] Put the other way, two-thirds of consumers don't trust the brands they buy. So, I'd say we have quite a bit of a gap to close. Companies that make ethics their top priority outperform those who don't.[2] A Cap Gemini study says that "by focusing on the values that matter to the consumer, CP [consumer products] companies will naturally increase the value of the company. Through emotive marketing, consumers find them-selves leaning toward choosing their product over another."[3] As is the case with purpose, there may or may not be watertight correla-tions with causation here, but shouldn't this be a fundamental as-pect for every marketer to be and do?

Marketing is, unfortunately, viewed as some kind of a con game by a large chunk of the population. And there is a good reason for it. It's largely the doing of the marketing community itself, the kind of practices they have been following over the decades.

Let's take a look at a few of these, which I will analyze as an in-formed consumer.

My wife buys some rather expensive moisturizing creams. The package design is very aesthetic, highly functional, and very appeal-ing. But it is also very deceptive. The glass jar looks fairly decent in size, but the inside bottom of the jar is far higher than the outside bottom of the jar. In other words, from the outside, the jar appears to contain a lot more than the jar's actual capacity. Is this a fair practice or a deceptive practice? My wife loves the product but hates the company and the brand. I asked a few friends of hers their opinions, and they answer, "These companies think we are stupid. After we discover that the bottom is raised and the capacity is really much smaller, we feel let down. And we hate the company for cheat-ing us. And if we have a good alternative, we will shift in a heart-beat." To them, this is a dishonest brand from a dishonest company.

Then there's the problem of false claims. A vast number of food supplements have been found to not have the ingredients they claim to have. Likewise, they have unhealthy ingredients they have not disclosed. That's an example of intentional wrong labeling, ir-respective of what local laws allow them to get away with.

Let me give you another example. My hometown is Cincin-nati. I travel frequently to and from Cincinnati to New York. When I book air tickets, I am horrified that most of the time the price between New York and Cincinnati is more expensive than between New York and Los Angeles, though the distance from New York to LA is more than two and a half times that of New

York to Cincinnati. Likewise, many times, I find that the ticket prices from New York to Cincinnati are more than New York to London, New York to Paris, and New York to Rome. No, we are not talking about the transcontinental tickets being low. We are talking about hyper pricing the tickets to Cincinnati. There may be very legitimate reasons for this kind of a crazy pricing structure—but, to consumers, it looks unfair and unethical.

So, what happens? Websites like Skiplagged have come up to show you holes in the airline's algorithms. If you don't have any checked baggage, you book your tickets to Chicago or LAX from New York on flights that have a stopover in Cincinnati. You simply walk off the plane in Cincinnati. What kind of a system have we come to? Do we need apps to beat companies at their game? This is the right kind of primordial mix, in which disruption led by intense necessity will come about and alter the status quo.

Take the entire concept of mail-in rebates. The business model of mail-in rebates was built upon the fact that consumers have inertia and are forgetful. Therefore, they will never, or rarely ever, claim the discount or the rebate. The entire program is designed to be that way. Knowing full well that consumers won't be sending in their mail-in rebate coupons, between forgetfulness, misplacing those stupid coupons, or sheer inertia, are the companies being smart or simply exploitative?

What about outright false claims or claims made that are legally sustainable but totally untrue in spirit? Is it okay to beguile consumers just because you can find a legal loophole? For example, a friend of mine who is obsessed with buying and eating only organic and natural foods went to one such store and bought an organic, natural yogurt. I took it from his hand and started reading the contents—it had ingredients like food starch, gelatin, carmine (food coloring), pectin . . . I was amazed and he was appalled! He was deeply disappointed that, when he read the label that proclaimed it to be natural and organic, there was anything else in the product other than yogurt, pure and simple.

Where do we draw the line between being a smart business practitioner and being a con artist? Shouldn't integrity and ethics be at the core of our practice? Can't we be successful without employing exploitative, deceptive, or misleading tactics?

DATA ETHICS

I've talked a lot about the concept of trust in this book. And I've talked a lot about data. There's an important intersection between the two. Just because Quantum Marketing depends on the aggressive use of data, that doesn't mean that data collection and usage is in itself reckless or exploitative. Trust, data, and ethics can all live in the same house. As an industry, we need to reset our priorities around data, particularly around data ethics.

Data ethics is about responsible, transparent, and fair use of data, with a strong sense of accountability. The World Federation of Advertisers has brilliantly summarized data ethics into a pithy statement: "There should not be a gap between what we could do with data and what we should do with data."[4]

In a conversation, Stephan Loerke, CEO of WFA, mentioned to me, "Data ethics has become a paradigm-shifting challenge that can be solved only when marketers make a mind shift from data first to people first. This needs everyone in the marketing ecosystem, from brands to ad tech to agencies to publishers, to come together so there is a sustainable future rooted in doing the right thing by the consumer."

ETHICS CREEP AND BRAND KARMA

Ethics and integrity transcend marketing. Breaches seep into every aspect of our lives, and scarily so. For example, when I have my car serviced, the service center calls me with a list of repairs and parts the car needs, though the car is not that old and has low mileage. I am not knowledgeable in this field, so I can't push back beyond asking some commonsense questions, to which they have ready and technical answers. I grudgingly permit them to go ahead and then pay up meekly. I am left with a feeling that my ignorance is being exploited. In fact, this experience is apparently so prevalent that now there is a product called FIXD, which when plugged into a car, supposedly shows what exactly is wrong, so the consumer will know if their car service center is cheating. The video on their site, at the time of writing this book, is titled "Never Be Ripped Off by Mechanics Again."[5] So products are being launched to protect you from being cheated by other brands, companies, or commercial entities.

I can go on and on with examples of practices that consumers don't like, practices that make them feel like brands are either tricking them, deceiving them, exploiting them, or gouging them.

This is further exacerbated by the fake news, political dramas, biased media vehicles, and corrupt government officials. No wonder there is a huge trust deficit all around.

As marketers, our livelihood depends on consumers. So why do we cheat them?

Know this: if consumers feel they have been wronged, companies and marketers are doing something incorrectly. Correct the model or correct the perception, or someone else will come and disrupt the hell out of your company.

Now let's set aside consumers for a change. What about within our industry itself? Significant allegations about agencies receiving kickbacks from media publishers were raised in the K2 Intelligence report that came out in 2016, commissioned by the Association of National Advertisers.[6] The report received a lot of scathing commentary, but as we speak, the US Justice Department is investigating these allegations, quite aggressively, as they must.

Today, society is replete with distrust. When competing media channels get a piece of data, the very same piece of data, they can have diametrically opposite interpretations, commentaries, and conclusions. Consumers are at a total loss of what to believe and what not to.

When artificial intelligence starts manifesting in a big way everywhere, it will aggravate the situation even more, by bringing in fake photos, fake videos, fake voices, and fake everything. For example, there are already AI-created videos in circulation of people gushing positively about their political rivals. AI creates photos of people and context so realistic it is impossible to tell that they are not real. The concept of visual evidence, which we rely on in our judicial system, goes out the window. Same thing with voice. It can be replicated very easily—the tone, diction, accent, and modulation.

WHAT DO WE DO IN THIS QUANTUM CHAOS?

Quantum Marketers must first realize that trust will be a gigantic competitive advantage. They have to focus on diligently and consistently building trust behind their brand. And they have to weed out things that erode it. The relevance and importance of brands in people's lives is on the wane. Against this backdrop, the brand that is trusted will stand tall for a long time. So, it is up to the marketers to build that trust.

We should follow straightforward practices, in spirit, word, and deed. Deceptive practices, whether advertising or pricing or packaging, will be sniffed out by the consumers from a mile away. And when they do it, will they be committed to such brands? They will always find alternatives, even if you think this brand has a monopoly.

Our advertisements have to be authentic and truthful. Don't miss opportunities to advertise and connect, but don't lead with opportunism. A beverage brand got rapped on its knuckles when they jumped in, opportunistically, about a social issue. When a brand is seen as being not authentic but merely taking advantage of a social issue, there is no advantage for the brand. One negative perception about your brand probably takes ten positive perceptions to be created before people can forget or forgive. Why get into that kind of situation?

Consumers appreciate truthfulness. Be bold and truthful in your product communication. No misrepresentation. Don't use fine print as the prime strategy.

As marketers, we have a lot of power to influence and shape culture. And to build the right role models. We can shape the perceptions and direction of society. That awesome power comes with the responsibility to do what is right by society. Charity begins at home. A marketer must first be ethical in their own practices before advising others on how to do things ethically.

Marketers should also look at all their partners and hold them accountable. Whether it is agencies or publishers or other partners and vendors, they should make sure that their practices are ethical. For example, sports sponsorships are a $46 billion global business,[7] but over time, several sports have been plagued by corruption and scandalous player behavior around the world. In fact, Interpol has seen so much sports corruption that it has published an advisory on spotting it and dealing with it.[8] As marketers, we should hold these various organizations' feet to the fire, because, at the end of the day, it is our marketing dollars that fund the sport big-time.

We have to be transparent. We should not rely on poor practices like baiting and switching. We should not drown consumers with terms and conditions we know they won't read, yet make them click to agree, which they'll do out of sheer helplessness or tedium. We must look at every consumer contact and interaction as an opportunity to not just sell or influence their preference in itself, but to engender trust.

As a Quantum Marketer, be a consumer and a decent human being, first and foremost. Don't do to the consumer what you don't want to be done to you. Treat the consumer the way you want to be treated.

Respect the privacy of consumers. A brand has no right to snoop, and without consumers' explicit permission, to sell. I am a big proponent of simplification of the privacy laws. I do support the federal laws in the United States and Europe's GDPR. But nothing is better than self-regulation and having an ethical North Star.

Marketers have to own and uphold the brand promise. We have to deliver through a delightful consumer experience. We have to give the rightly configured product and charge the right way. And we have to make sure that there is no deception, lying, cheating, or exploitation.

Is this naive? Absolutely not. The Fifth Paradigm is going to be a different world. The same old, same old won't work. The expectations and parameters are totally different. To succeed, marketers must live up to these levels. For example, if there is something negative about your product, it's better to declare it up front. If not, someone will start talking about it on social media and the result will be a PR firestorm. I have seen some web-based products being developed that look at the various product claims, summarize the falsities, and troll the brands with facts. We haven't even seen the beginning of this yet.

Ethics should be contagious. It's extremely critical that marketers inculcate the spirit of ethics and integrity in their own teams. They have to make sure that things are inclusive. They have to make sure that there is gender balance. They have to embrace and enable diversity.

Let's revisit the sports example. There is a tremendous amount of disparity that persists in the support of women's sports vs. men's. If a brand is a sponsor, they should insist on both inclusiveness and gender balance. What is interesting is how much of a gender imbalance exists, across the board, in spite of the fact that more than 75 percent of all purchase decisions are made by women across categories from health care to payments.

As is the case with the rest of our lives, doing bad things might tend to give a positive advantage in the immediate or short term. But it will catch up in the long run, for sure. This is what I call brand karma. Embrace an ethical approach and operate with complete integrity, and the team and the brand will blossom, slowly and surely. And it will make all the difference in the Fifth Paradigm.

CHAPTER 17

Marketing through Crisis

The pandemic woke and shook every businessperson and every marketer around the world. In the last few decades, no one has witnessed the kind of havoc that COVID-19 wreaked around the world. Everything came to a grinding halt, leading to a situation in which not just some companies but entire industries were shut down.

Hundreds of thousands of people died. Millions were laid off. And millions more were furloughed. A large number of companies filed for bankruptcies, and hundreds of thousands, if not millions, of small businesses closed down permanently. Companies' revenues were severely impacted. Not surprisingly, marketing budgets got substantially slashed, if not totally eliminated, across the board.

Oil prices touched negative territory. People were quarantined in their homes. Social distancing and remote working became the norm. People's lives were disrupted at a level unimagined by even the most surreal writers.

If you had been asked to create a crisis of unprecedented scale, expense, and impact, you couldn't have outdone the "coronacrisis." And if you are a student of crisis management, you couldn't have dreamt up a better crisis to learn from, in which every single aspect of the world's ecosystem was impacted. In some ways, there is no better teacher for future preparedness than the coronacrisis and its lessons.

People have been forced to alter their lifestyles for the shutdown period, and those changes will have a profound impact. Some will stay with people as new behaviors. Consumers may not go back to all pre-crisis scenarios. For example, online shopping became the new habit of many who had never shopped online before. People were literally forced to try out new ways (online shopping, streaming video channels), new products (hand sanitizers), new ways of interacting socially (Zoom parties), new ways to work (remotely), a new focus on health and well-being (yoga, meditation, health foods, and supplements), new interpretations of luxury (being and doing as opposed to possessing), and so on. All this will leave a permanent mark on how people will live their lives in future. And, of course, marketing has to adjust to this new norm. This is yet another manifestation of massive changes and transformation that characterize the Fifth Paradigm as well as Quantum Marketing. COVID-19 had no precedent and there was no playbook.

Many experts say that this will not be the last of this kind of pandemic. They say that this pandemic or something else can come at us in waves. Whether those events will have the scale of this recent pandemic is a question. What's not in question is that crises will keep happening. Whether it is a health crisis, economic crisis, cybersecurity crisis, political crisis, humanitarian crisis, natural disaster crisis—crises can happen in so many forms. It is critical that marketers stay prepared to tackle whatever is thrown at them. If crisis is going to be part and parcel of life, crisis management will also need to be part and parcel of life. Whether the next crisis is big or small, marketers need to maintain a state of preparedness. When, not if, the crisis materializes, they should be ready to press the buttons to switch their strategy, plans, and tactics to contain any damage. Thus, they need to appropriately reposition and protect their brand and business against harm.

Here are a few points to focus on.

RISK MANAGEMENT

As I have stated, marketing has to deal with a number of risks. Historically, marketers would typically treat as the main risks some blowback of a poorly conceived campaign or a PR disaster. And they would tackle them as and when they happened. But since marketing is going to be heavily enabled by technology and data, new types of risks will emerge that need to be addressed appropriately. Then, there is reputational risk, financial risk, intellectual property risk, compliance risk, legal risk, consumer privacy risk, and on and on, each of which can blow up so big that they can blast a company out of business.

It is absolutely imperative for marketers to begin being responsible for risk management. It can be a structural solution, like having a risk management professional embedded within marketing or supporting it fully from the outside.

Most large and mid-sized companies have a risk matrix or a risk heat map at a company level that they present to their boards. They have a process by which a company identifies all the risks they may be subjected to, the probability of it happening, the likely impact if it does indeed happen, and so on. Visually, it lays out all the risks and draws focus on the key ones. And they typically have action plans to mitigate or respond to these risks.

Marketers need to plot risk maps, and crisis management plans should always be updated and kept ready. Should disaster strike, the management team should know exactly who does what and when.

Figure 10 is the sample risk heat map template. In this risk heat map, different risks are plotted based on their likelihood of materializing and the impact they can have if they materialize.

The risks on the top right are the ones that can break the bank, so marketers need to watch them like a hawk. Not only that, risks are dynamic. Marketers need to regularly reassess the risks with all their partners and determine if the risk's position in the map shifts. The idea is not to produce a colorful chart for fun, but to present all the risks in one view. This will help everyone involved understand the risk profiles, prioritize the ones to address, and prepare plans in advance to either avoid, mitigate, or contain the risks. For each risk, marketers need to create a mitigation plan on the one hand, which is more proactive, and a containment plan on the other, which is how the damage is minimized. These plans would include identifying the people on the team who are responsible to keep a sharp eye on the risk, the key indicators that need to be monitored to know that the risk has materialized or is materializing, the containment tactics, and so on.

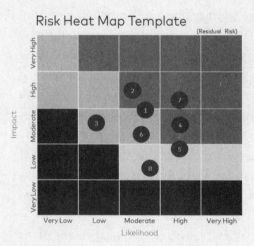

FIGURE 10

PURPOSE IN A CRISIS

In good times, it is easy to propound about the purpose-driven nature of an organization and for the CEOs of those companies to make eloquent speeches about how their company is committed to pursue its North Star. When a crisis hits, however, the purpose may not be pursued and the company gets distracted.

In reality, purpose should be the North Star, and the North Star doesn't change position. It gives direction when one is lost. Irrespective of floods, typhoons, or fires, figuratively (and even literally) speaking, the purpose remains steadfast. What does change, though, is how a marketer acts on that purpose using a different set of tactics and strategies that are more appropriate to the situation at hand. One needs to keep plowing through and forward, irrespective of the times, good or bad.

SERVING VERSUS SELLING

There is a time to sell and there is a time to serve. In normal times, a marketer would want to aggressively, continually, and properly market and sell the company's products and services to the customers and consumers. But a crisis is not a time to sell. A crisis is the time to serve.

Crisis is certainly not the time to pursue sales ambitions. It is so rightly said that a friend in need is a friend indeed. If a brand sticks with people and serves them during their tough and troubled times, when the tide turns and the good times come back, they will stick with this brand.

Crisis is not the time to be opportunistic. Crisis is when trust gets built or broken. If a brand seems to be self-serving, opportunistic, or, worse, exploitative, that trust is broken. Serving customers during crisis builds lasting trust. And that is truly Priceless.

DON'T BE EXPLOITATIVE

Marketers and companies should not exploit their customers and consumers in any situation. During a crisis, there may be a shortfall of some items, or people may need some items very badly. There may be an easy opportunity to jack up the price and gouge the consumers. They will buy it still, because they may not have a choice. But they will remember. When good times come, or when the brand needs them, they will show the brand the way out.

I experienced this, as a consumer, during the 2020 coronacrisis. Since I was in a locked down mode and was working from home, I wanted to buy a stand for my tablet. The price was $61, which was fine. But I fell off my chair when the price for shipping was shown as $211! In normal times, they would do free shipping for orders more than $25. Likewise, I ordered some hand sanitizers, which I could buy only at eight times the normal price! This is exploitation and price gouging, pure and simple. And will I ever visit that online retailer again?

Trust is a huge factor to build and nurture. Foolish short-term tactics that are unfair and exploitative will never serve a brand in good stead.

CRISIS COMMUNICATION

At times of crisis, the PR or communications team will play an absolutely crucial role. Nothing is more important than to let all key stakeholders, both internal or external, know exactly what is happening, what the brand is doing about it, and why they should feel comfortable that the brand is doing the right things to control as much of the situation as possible. This is extremely important.

It starts with internal communications, where everyone is kept informed, not just the CEO and the management committee, but the entire company. That will help people avoid panic or guessing and rumor mongering. Everyone needs all the relevant facts and everyone should be operating from the same page. A company's employees are its best advocates during a normal situation, and even more so during a crisis.

For external stakeholders, a clear strategy needs to be mapped out, a proactive outreach needs to be made, and appropriate information shared. Leverage influencers must advocate for the brand. This is influencer marketing of a different flavor.

Many times, I have seen communications experts avoid a social media war. They feel, rightly so, that when a brand jumps in to defend and clarify, it only aggravates the situation and prolongs the news cycle. So, they suggest that it is best to stay on the sidelines and hope that social media will catch the next shiny penny and the company will be off the radar.

A better approach, often, is for the company to assert itself and vigorously clarify, rather than running and hiding. A brand needs to be assertive. If the company made mistakes, it needs to own up, apologize, and let the consumers know what it is doing to rectify the situation. If the company stays silent, social media audiences will become the judge and jury. If the company has not messed up, it should clarify. It is a smart approach to get on top of the issue, jump into the conversation, and make sure that people hear the company's side of the story. It is important to build advocacy for the brand during normal times, so those advocates come to the rescue during crises.

CRISIS MARKETING BUDGETS

A crisis will almost certainly affect the marketing budget. When society is in turmoil, consumption gets affected, and revenues go down. When revenues go down, it is only natural that expenses are cut. Typically, marketing is one of the larger expense lines, so it is no surprise that the CEO and CFO will look to cut marketing budgets. It is important that marketers don't feel like victims but see the big picture and not attempt to hoard money. When I talk about how the trust between the CFO and marketing needs to be built, these are the occasions when a marketer should step up and demonstrate maturity on the one hand, appreciation of the company's situation on the other, and do what is right by the company.

During a crisis, marketers should bring about order and drive focus—what to prioritize and what to deprioritize. You cannot do all the good activities you want to do during good times when there is a dearth of money during the bad.

DON'T GO DARK

While it might be necessary to pull back marketing budgets during a crisis, it is important not to go dark. It is in times of crisis when a brand needs to assert itself and stay appropriately visible.

It is vital to be very sensitive to consumer or customer sentiment and not be tone deaf. As the old saying goes, even when you say the right things, it is important that you say them right. Obviously, we need the right messaging strategy, the right narrative, the right tone, and most importantly, the right timing. If any one of these is lacking, it will paint a very different picture than the intended message. It can sound the death knell if a brand is seen as either being insincere or self-serving.

A word of caution on humor. Marketers need to be very careful about deploying humor during a crisis. Humor, if done well, can work most times, but it's less likely to when people are hurting. Humor can be mistaken for mockery or tone deafness.

Another caution: the sea of sameness. As witnessed during the COVID-19 crisis, nearly every brand has exactly the same set of themes and eerily similar messages—thanking health-care workers, for example. There's danger of getting lost if a brand joins that band wagon. It all becomes one indistinguishable mass with no attribution to the respective brands whatsoever.

STAY IN CLOSE TOUCH WITH YOUR PEOPLE

Marketers cannot overcommunicate with their teams and agency partners during a crisis. It is vital the team knows their managers and company management are there for them. The team members and the agencies need to see management as visible and accessible. Management is a high-contact sport, so it is important for the managers to reach out to the team members frequently. Managers and management are respected when they are truthful and transparent. Management should not panic. They should encourage everyone to give feedback and, of course, be receptive to that feedback.

PLAYBOOK

There are a number of crisis management playbooks out there from which a marketer can build their own. In combination with the risk heat map, detailed risk mitigation and containment plans should be prepared in advance. The teams need to be trained well, including in war room situations.

The speed and scale of the Fifth Paradigm will inevitably result in its fair share of crises. Expect them and be ready to tackle them.

TO SUMMARIZE . . .

➤ Crises will come at us very certainly. Whether the next crisis is big or small, marketers always need to maintain a state of preparedness. When, not if, the crisis materializes, they should be ready to switch their strategy, plans, and tactics to contain any damage.

➤ It is imperative to have a risk management focus within marketing that creates and updates risk heat maps, crisis management plans, and crisis management training programs for team members.

➤ Crisis is not the time to pursue sales ambitions. It is so rightly said that a friend in need is a friend indeed, which means that if a brand sticks with people and serves them during their tough and troubled times, when the tide turns and the good times come back, they will stick with the brand.

➤ Internal communications are critical to crisis management. A company's employees are its best advocates during normal times and even more so during a crisis.

➤ While it might be necessary to pull back marketing budgets during a crisis, it is important not to go dark. It is actually in times of crisis that a brand needs to assert itself and stay appropriately visible.

CHAPTER 18

The Quantum CMO

I start this chapter with a great deal of hope and optimism. While I have made the case that marketing is under existential risk, I also have every confidence that it is poised for a renaissance. That is because marketing can be a powerful accelerator of business momentum and a significant competitive advantage to a company. In other words, marketing can be a true force multiplier.

It is important for marketers to demonstrate to CEOs and other senior business leaders what marketing can bring to the table, the value it can unlock for their organizations. They need to be shown the terrific competitive edge that marketing can create for their company, even as it can help fuel their business and power their performance. They should be shown how marketing can enhance profitability, increase customer acquisition, help drive retention, and enhance overall reputation. They should be shown how marketing can ensure a company's short-, medium- and long-term progress.

As we enter the Fifth Paradigm, now more than ever, marketing's role is incredibly valuable and very powerful for a company's success. The world is going to turn upside down in the Fifth Paradigm. We see new technologies coming in a torrent. The amount of data grows exponentially, analytics become pervasive and all powerful, AI brings extraordinary capabilities to the fore, and the democratization of all these capabilities brings them within the reach of every company, big and small. Product parity and significant price wars are the norm, with disruption of every industry. How do companies differentiate their brands, products, services, campaigns, and offerings? With consumer attention span shrinking, with all the information overload, how do companies cut through the clutter, engage with the consumers, and persuade them to choose their offerings? With trust eroding in every aspect of consumers' lives, how will companies build trusting and lasting brand affinities and preferences? The challenges ahead are simply of an unprecedented—Quantum—magnitude.

What will differentiate a company's offerings is not product design or functionality. Not price. Not simplistic and copycat promotions. The role of marketing is going to be absolutely and mightily critical in this imminent future. And, scarily, a lot of companies don't yet realize this. If the marketing function is tasked with clear expectations and empowered to bring them about, it can indeed make a huge, positive difference. Marketing is at a point of inflection, and the opportunity ahead is truly once in a lifetime. If embraced, it can take off from here brilliantly. Or it can totally implode. Here is where the Quantum CMO comes in. And here are what characterize Quantum CMOs:

1. Quantum CMOs are like Leonardo Da Vinci. They are multifaceted and multitalented, excelling at the art, science, and the technology of marketing. They are both right brained and left brained, creative and analytical.

2. Quantum CMOs are primarily business leaders who understand the business. They deeply appreciate how their business makes money. They are true general managers, with deep marketing expertise, as opposed to being pure marketing specialists.

3. They are strong leaders. They demonstrate a confidence and assertiveness that comes not only out of personality but from understanding the business dynamics along with having a command over the field of marketing. They can connect the dots between the two.

4. Quantum CMOs are incredibly knowledgeable about the foundational and classical aspects of marketing. Quantum CMOs understand the basics of human psychology, sociology, and anthropology. They grasp every one of the 4 Ps of marketing. They know, in depth, about pricing strategies and price elasticity, brand positioning, purchase funnels, advertising models, agency workings, packaging design, how promotions work, how to negotiate sponsorships and partnerships and leverage them fully, how to inspire and drive marketing, how to measure the ROIs of their campaigns in general and marketing investment overall, how to manage the marketing processes most effectively, how to coordinate the myriad things that chug away in the workshop of marketing.

5. Quantum CMOs also have a deep appreciation of the contemporary and emerging fields of marketing. They know data-driven marketing cold. They are on top of performance marketing. They have an innate ability for experiential marketing. They know neuro marketing. They know behavioral economics. They have a good grasp of all the emerging fields of marketing. More so, they know data and digital technologies, as these are the two primary engines that will supercharge marketing into the future. The big difference in the Fifth Paradigm is that data will be literally exploding, thanks to proliferating sensors and the Internet of Things, which, combined with the incredible power of artificial intelligence, is going to be a total game changer. Quantum CMOs understand all of this, so they don't put at risk their ability to lead.

6. Quantum CMOs are technologically savvy. They aren't necessarily deep subject matter experts, but at least they have enough comprehension and working knowledge to be able to ask the right questions and see through any fluff in the answers. They visualize and inspire the teams to think about how those new technologies can be used to give their companies a leg up over everybody else, not just the competitors in their own category but across all categories. These days, brands don't compete just within their category for a share of the mind and heart.

7. Quantum CMOs are on top of connecting the dots between marketing activities and business outcomes. They manage significant budgets, and that comes with a responsibility and accountability to drive results. The Quantum CMO's CEO or CFO clearly understands what exactly marketing is doing for the company and how it is adding value at various levels, how it helps grow top-line and bottom-line results. Marketing can and should play a stupendous role in the company's growth agenda.

8. Quantum CMOs are inspiring leaders with a big vision. I speak of vision because everything is in a massive transformational phase. Visualize what the possibilities could be. Quantum CMOs see beyond the horizon; they don't just react to the future coming at them fast but shape that future. And that will provide an unfair competitive advantage, which is exactly what is needed. Quantum CMOs have big thinking, big vision, an ability to get the big picture when everything seems to be very chaotic, and use that to get excited, inspired, and drive a vision for the company that is going to be fantastic.

9. Quantum CMOs are strong, empathetic leaders, because they are literally driving teams through this transformational phase, which is not easy. People can find themselves floundering and at a loss, with all the external and internal changes coming so fast. Quantum CMOs guide people through the churn, paint a big vision and make it tangible, decode the chaos, simplify the big picture, stand with them in the trenches, lead them successfully through challenges, keep up their morale, inspire them to be at their best, and make them feel a part of the winning team.

10. Quantum CMOs are evangelists for marketing, particularly if they are in companies that are not marketing driven. They are assertive, confident, able to reach out across the aisle to their various peers, get their emotional buy-in, and demonstrate the power of marketing and the difference it can make to the business. They enable a cultural transformation within the company and help the company see the possibilities of what marketing can do, not just by painting a rosy future but by demonstrating tangible outcomes. They speak the language of the CEOs and the CFOs and are thus successful in the organization. And because the historical experience at most of these companies with marketing has not been fantastic, they demonstrate, not just propound, the power of marketing. They go the extra mile to prove things. They, in effect, rebrand marketing and drive a change in how it is perceived within the company. They build a credible case not only for why the company should continue to invest in marketing but why they should be embracing marketing as a key business driver and a significant competitive advantage for the company.

11. Quantum CMOs have tremendous curiosity and agility. Many of us have gone to management schools, many moons ago. Life has changed a lot since then. Quantum CMOs aren't still stuck in an earlier paradigm of marketing; they aren't anachronisms. They keep pace with all the changes, rather than become obsolete. They re-educate themselves, learn about the latest and the greatest, stay at the cutting edge. They devote time regularly to read about an emerging topic, take mentoring sessions from subject matter experts, read white papers on potential applications, and so on. Yes, Quantum CMOs put in the time and effort to stay up to speed.

12. Quantum CMOs have a global mind-set. Many CMOs, particularly from the United States, seem to have a very US-centric approach. So much is happening outside of the US, often a lot more than in the US. Quantum CMOs adopt a global perspective and literally make the world their oyster. They try to get a stint or two in countries other than their own, to understand and get a first-hand feel for how cultures can manifest with different nuances, how workforce mind-sets are so vastly different from culture to culture, how legal and regulatory environments vary, and how various principles manifest in different cultures with very different societal composition.

13. Quantum CMOs are team builders. Their team members have deeper experiences in some areas, but may not in other areas. It's almost impossible to find ready-made talent terrific at everything; so, Quantum CMOs get people who have a solid aptitude, with a great attitude, with a terrific work ethic, with a brilliant cultural mind-set and fit for the company, and who are curious and agile. Then, they enable these people to learn and cross-train, whether through self-studies, online programs, group training sessions, colleges, working for other departments, job rotations, or whatever else that helps them on their learning journey.

14. Quantum CMOs view marketing as a customer-facing function, that they are important ambassadors of the company. Quantum CMOs are out there in the field, meeting distributors, sales colleagues, team members, clients and prospects, agency and other partners, the local media, the local marketing and advertising bodies, other CMOs in those markets, and so on. They continuously look for and drive opportunities to enable marketing to go up to the next level. Nothing is more insightful than seeing everything in the field and interacting with clients and peers, and inspiring them about the company's products and brands.

15. Quantum CMOs understand that their roles don't end with growing and protecting the brand and the company. They realize that they wield an unbelievable level of marketing power and influence and can make a difference. When joining hands with others in the marketing community, and across the entire marketing ecosystem, they make an enormous difference to the society at large. Collectively, we as marketers spend well in excess of $1 trillion every year. We shape cultural norms, aspirations, role models—we have a huge influence. This power and influence comes with responsibility, the responsibility to do good in society, not just because it's fashionable or is expected, but because it is the right thing to do. Quantum CMOs focus on any area that is relevant to the company and good for the society, such as making the internet a safe space; making the planet safe for the future generations of all living things; eradicating hunger; finding cures for cancer. It is important to note that consumers want and insist that brands act for societal good. While that is an important reason, Quantum CMOs know that it is important to feel the need to do it from within. So, they are finely attuned with society or the community (after all, as sound marketers, they have a great grasp of the lives, living conditions, aspirations, and pain points of people) and have the sensibilities to empathize and act.

16. Quantum CMOs play an important role in formulating the regulatory environment, even as the brave new future is dawning, whether it is privacy, brand safety, agency transparency, or something else. A lot of fundamental and foundational areas of marketing are getting redefined. Quantum CMOs are actively involved in shaping those. They join the marketing community via the trade bodies like World Federation of Advertisers, the Association of National Advertisers, local marketing associations, or local advertising clubs. They absolutely play a part in helping to shape the policies and define the parameters for the industry.

17. Quantum CMOs are good partners. Not everything can be created and invented within a given company, nor can everything be done solely by CMOs and their teams. In fact, throughout my own career, I have found that most of the innovative ideas come from small, external companies. They are start-ups from Silicon Valley or elsewhere. They are hungry for business and are driven to succeed. I found it exceptionally beneficial to join hands with them. We could jump-start innovation and go to market with new ideas, while at the same time, providing scale and market power to these start-ups.

18. Quantum CMOs are agency realists. One of my bosses, very early in my career, once told me that agencies are not our servants but our equal partners. I've remembered that message my entire life, and I think it is the right mind-set for the future. Quantum CMOs set an example to the team by always treating the agency partners as truly equal partners. They may pay the bill, but agencies help create magic. Even as the agency models are changing, even as the various consulting firms are getting into the agency business, even as agencies are being brought in house, I find the agencies are invaluable partners in our march toward success. They are a natural extension of my team and they have a vested interest in our success. Both of us have exactly the same objective: to create magical work that all of us would feel very proud of, work that would make a positive difference in the marketplace for our brand, and work that advances the company's business. Quantum CMOs understand that agencies need to feel inspired and that their best creativity will come through partnership, not by terrorizing them, threatening to shift the business elsewhere, or incessantly cutting down fees.

19. Quantum CMOs take care of their health. They are under constant pressure, like any other C-suite executive. But they know that if they are not in optimal health, they will be unable to perform at their best. Their physical health is very critical, particularly more so because they travel a lot, flitting across time zones, eating all kinds of food at all different times, attending customer events, and so forth. They put their body through a lot. But, they are responsible for their bodies and need to have a healthy routine, healthy diet, and adequate sleep. They are in a peak mental state to keep their creative juices flowing. One of the things I have found most helpful is meditation. Meditating for half an hour a day can not only give peace of mind and calmness, but it can profoundly transform one's creativity. Quantum CMOs feed the mind by reading a lot.

20. Quantum CMOs have not only a high intelligence or emotional quotient, they have a high creative quotient (CQ). And to borrow from Ajay Banga, Executive Chairman of Mastercard, they have a high decency quotient (DQ). Quantum CMOs are decent human beings, first and foremost. They treat everyone, be it team members, colleagues across different functions, vendors, or agency partners, with respect and fairness. Quantum CMOs have a good mix of IQ, EQ, CQ, and DQ.

21. Quantum CMOs feel happy, energized about, and look forward to their work, or they change their way of going about it or move. They know that life is too precious to be wasted on unnecessary drudgery or living every day with insecurity. The world is full of opportunities for talented people—they know they can always find their best match. In the Fifth Paradigm, the competition is going to be brutal, and the world of business will be going through tectonic changes. The need for marketing will be felt and realized, so Quantum CMOs will have ample opportunities.

One final point, this one for CEOs. If you are planning to hire a CMO, please put in place someone who knows and is experienced in marketing. Marketing cannot be run by pure common sense. It takes a fine blend of the art and science of marketing. It needs a person keenly sensitive to nuances of feelings and with a gift to articulate the abstract. Years of marketing experience trains marketers along those lines and gives them a judgment that goes beyond algorithms. Your CMO needs to be an evangelist for the function within the rest of the company and build strong bridges with others. Someone cannot simply wing it with common sense or general management background alone. Marketing is not just about managing people, processes, and optimizing investment; it is about inspiring your internal teams and external partners to create magic for the company. It is not just creativity for creativity's sake, but it is creativity to drive the business and build a huge competitive advantage. In a world where everything will be at parity—be it product functionality, capabilities, supply chain efficiencies, or whatever—you need marketing to differentiate and distinguish your offerings and build lasting trust, aspiration, and affinity for your brand. You need someone with knowledge, experience, versatility, a business mind-set, and a bunch of other factors I listed in the preceding twenty-one points. You need a Quantum CMO.

I am confident that marketing will get back to where it belongs: in the spotlight, in a place where it's delivering and driving businesses, where people are enjoying themselves, having fun. As practicing marketers, let's also help with building the future generations of Quantum Marketers. It's critical we share our knowledge with the universities, where new marketers are being developed. We need to make sure that they are taught the right things, aided by the right tools, led by awesome professors. So, let's give serious projects to these students as they go through their internships instead of giving them inane and menial survey tasks. Let's give the professors case studies, based on the real work happening in the real world. The academicians and the practitioners should frequently connect and learn from one another. It will be a nice idea for some of the professors to spend some time with the CMOs and observe them in action. Likewise, it will be great for the marketers to deliver lectures at a class or two.

Thank you for staying with me through these eighteen chapters. I hope you found it useful. You may not agree or subscribe to my point of view on everything, but if this book can serve as a wake-up call, thought starter, or inspiration at some level, my purpose in writing it is served. You can always reach me at raja.rajamannar@quantummarketing.com or follow me on twitter @RajaRajamannar or on LinkedIn.

I wish you all the very best!

Thank you!

Acknowledgments

I have always been thinking about the transforming future of marketing and have been sharing my thoughts over the last few years in bits and pieces at various forums, in addition to bringing them to bear in my role at Mastercard and in the previous companies where I worked. In the middle of 2019, I began writing the concept for this book, trying to capture the essence of my industry experience of more than three decades but also, more importantly, my vision, perspectives, and concepts about the future. I was fortunate that Scott Hoffman, my literary agent, saw the promise in the book and gave me invaluable suggestions and helped me navigate this passion project to bring it to fruition. I am very grateful to Scott!

I want to thank Sara Kendrick, senior editor at HarperCollins Leadership, for challenging my hypotheses, concepts, and assertions—that made the outcome so much better. I feel fortunate to have had her terrific insights and support throughout the process. I am also thankful to the other amazing folks working with HarperCollins Leadership—including Jeff Farr, David McNeill, and Ron Huizinga—for their excellent support. And I also want to thank Sicily Axton, who helped craft and follow through with the marketing and PR plans extremely well for launching the book.

I am grateful to John Gaffney, who did an outstanding job of assisting me throughout the making of this book.

I want to thank my peers and other industry leaders who have read my manuscript and given me valuable feedback and endorsement. Their effusively positive feedback kept me energetically going forward.

Finally, I want to thank my family, my teachers, my friends, and my colleagues over the years—they all have had a huge impact on who I am today, and I am grateful to them. And I feel grateful to my spiritual guru, Sri Parakala Swamy, for his guidance over the decades, and I dedicate this book to him.

Notes

PREFACE

1. "12 Ways CEOs Can Support Their Marketing Teams," *Forbes*, June 12, 2017. Accessed at https://www.forbes.com/sites/forbescommun icationscouncil/2017/06/12/12-ways-ceos-can-support-their -marketing-teams/#d5e67637859a.

CHAPTER 1

1. Stephanie Pappas, "Pompeii 'Wall Posts' Reveal Ancient Social Networks," Live Science, January 10, 2013. Accessed at https://www .livescience.com/26164-pompeii-wall-graffiti-social-networks.html.
2. https://www.coursehero.com/file/p305hjd/Bronze-plate-for -printing-an-advertisement-for-the-Liu-family-needle-shop-at/.
3. "The Ancient Origins and History of Modern Marketing and Advertising," LaFleur, July 26, 2016. Accessed at https://lafleur .marketing/blog/ancient-origins-history-modern-marketing -advertising/.
4. Amelia Lucas, "Burger King Sells Whoppers for a Penny at McDonald's Locations to Promote Its App," CNBC, December 4, 2018. Accessed at https://www.cnbc.com/2018/12/04/burger- king - sells-whoppers-for-a-penny-at-mcdonalds-locations.html.
5. "Vintage Dodge Ad, 1951," Pinterest, uploaded by Robert Stead. Accessed at https://www.pinterest.com/pin/285767538825843116/.
6. Becky Little, "When Cigarette Companies Used Doctors to Push Smoking," History.com, September 13, 2018 (updated September

11, 2019). Accessed at https://www.history.com/news/cigarette-ads
-doctors-smoking-endorsement.

7.   Ross Benes, "'The Beginning of a Giant Industry': An Oral History
of the First Banner Ad," Digiday, November 8, 2017. Accessed at
https://digiday.com/media/history-of-the-banner-ad/.

8.   Susan Young, "Getting the Message: How the Internet Is Changing
Advertising," Harvard Business School Working Knowledge, May
16, 2000. Accessed at https://hbswk.hbs.edu/archive/getting-the
-message-how-the-internet-is-changing-advertising.

9.   Susan Young, "Getting the Message: How the Internet Is Changing
Advertising." Harvard Business School Working Knowledge, May
16, 2000. Accessed at https://hbswk.hbs.edu/archive/getting-the
-message-how-the-internet-is-changing-advertising.

10.   Jeff Desjardins, "What Happens in an Internet Minute in 2019?"
Visual Capitalist, March 13, 2019. Accessed at https://www
.visualcapitalist.com/what-happens-in-an-internet-minute
-in-2019/.

11.   Quentin Fottrell, "People Spend Most of Their Waking Hours
Staring at Screens," Market Watch, August 4, 2018. Accessed at
https://www.marketwatch.com/story/people-are-spending-most
-of-their-waking-hours-staring-at-screens-2018-08-01.

12.   "Ellen's Oscar 'Selfie' Crashes Twitter, Breaks Record," CNBC,
March 3, 2014. Accessed at https://www.cnbc.com/2014/03/03
/ellens-oscar-selfie-crashes-twitter-breaks-record.html.

13.   Kaya Yurieff, "Snapchat Loses $1.3 Billion after Kylie Jenner
Tweet," CNN Business, February 23, 2018. Accessed at https://
money.cnn.com/2018/02/22/technology/snapchat-update-kylie
-jenner/index.html.

14.   "Programmatic Adspend to Exceed US$100bn for the First Time in
2019," Zenith, the ROI Agency, November 25, 2019. Accessed at
https://www.zenithmedia.com/programmatic-adspend-to-exceed
-us100bn-for-the-first-time-in-2019/.

15.   Laurie Sullivan, "Data Estimates 40% of All Media Spent Is
Wasted—How One Company Is Plugging the Holes," MediaPost,
September 23, 2019. Accessed at https://www.mediapost.com
/publications/article/340946/data-estimates-40-of-all-media-spend
-is-wasted-.html.

16.   Suzanne Vranica, "Ad Business Full of Nontransparent Practices,
Study Finds," Wall Street Journal, June 7, 2017. Accessed at https://

www.wsj.com/articles/ad-business-full-of-nontransparent
-practices-study-finds-1465303654.

17. Suzanne Vranica and Nicole Hong, "Federal Prosecutors Probe Ad
Industry's Media-Buying Practices," *Wall Street Journal*, September
27, 2018. Accessed at https://www.wsj.com/articles/federal
-prosecutors-probe-ad-industrys-media-buying-practices
-1538078020.

18. Devin Coldeway, "The California Consumer Privacy Act Officially
Takes Effect Today," TechCrunch, January 1, 2020. Accessed at
https://techcrunch.com/2020/01/01/the-california-consumer
-privacy-act-officially-takes-effect-today/.

CHAPTER 2

1. Darrell Etherington, "Amazon's Prime Air Drone Delivery Fleet
Gains FAA Approval for Trial Commercial Flights," *TechCrunch*,
August 31, 2020. Accessed at https://techcrunch.com/2020/08/31
/amazons-prime-air-drone-delivery-fleet-gains-faa-approval-for
-trial-commercial-flights/.

CHAPTER 3

1. Richard Whitman, "McCann Research Drives New ANA Talent
Recruitment Effort," MediaPost, November 14, 2019. Accessed at
https://www.mediapost.com/publications/article/343374/mccann
-research-drives-new-ana-talent-recruitment.html.

CHAPTER 4

1. "New Research Reveals Most Consumers Unaware of Financial
Data Collection Practices," The Clearing House, November 19,
2019. Accessed at https://www.theclearinghouse.org/payment
-systems/articles/2019/11/new-research-financial-data-collection
-practices-11-19-19.

2. Ray Walsh, "Organizations Sign Privacy International Petition
Criticizing Exploitive Pre-Installed Apps on Android," ProPrivacy,

January 9, 2020. Accessed at https://proprivacy.com/privacy-news /organizations-sign-privacy-international-petition.

3.   Eric Rosenbaum, "5 Biggest Risks of Sharing Your DNA with Consumer Genetic-Testing Companies," CNBC, June 16, 2019. Accessed at https://www.cnbc.com/2018/06/16/5-biggest-risks-of -sharing-dna-with-consumer-genetic-testing-companies.html.

4.   Whitney Ksiazek, Leslie Picker, and Nick Wells, "How Hedge Fund Investors are Makings Money Off the Data You're Giving Them for Free," CNBC, April 23, 2019. Accessed at https://www.cnbc .com/2019/04/23/how-hedge-funds-use-alternative-data-to-make -investments.html.

5.   Chelsea Bailey and Elizabeth Chuck, "Apple CEO Time Cook Slams Facebook: Privacy 'is a human right, it's a civil liberty'," NBC News, March 28, 2018. Accessed at https://www.nbcnews.com/tech/tech -news/apple-ceo-tim-cook-slams-facebook-privacy-human-right -it-n860816.

6.   "MyID Platform Enables a Trusted Digital ID Ecosystem," MYID Alliance webpage. Accessed at https://myidalliance.org/en/.

7.   Brave homepage. Accessed at https://brave.com.

8.   Jesse Hollington, "Hacker Who Tried to Blackmail Apple by Threatening to Delete 319 Million iCloud Accounts Gets Two-Year Sentence," iDrop News, December 26, 2019. Accessed at https:// www.idropnews.com/news/hacker-who-tried-to-blackmail-apple -by-threatening-to-delete-319-million-icloud-accounts-gets-two -year-sentence/125904/.

9.   Simon Fogg, "GDPR for Dummies: Simple GDPR Guide for Beginners," Termly, September 20, 2019. Accessed at https://termly .io/resources/articles/gdpr-for-dummies/.

10. "Privacy by Design GDPR," Privacy Trust, 2018. Accessed at https:// www.privacytrust.com/gdpr/privacy-by-design-gdpr.html.

CHAPTER 5

1.   Mario Klingermann homepage. Accessed at http://quasimondo .com.

2.   "An Interview with Scott Eaton," Direct Digital. Accessed at https:// www.direct-digital.com/en/case-study/interview-scott-eaton.

3.   Refik Anadol homepage. Accessed at http://refikanadol.com.

4.   Karen Gilchrist, "Chatbots Expected to Cut Business Costs by $8

Billion by 2022," CNBC, May 9, 2017. Accessed at https://www
.cnbc.com/2017/05/09/chatbots-expected-to-cut-business-costs-by
-8-billion-by-2022.html.

5. "JWT's 'The Next Rembrandt' Wins Two Grand Prix and an
    Innovation Lion at Cannes," IBB online, 2016. Accessed at https://
    www.lbbonline.com/news/jwts-the-next-rembrandt-wins-two
    -grand-prix-and-an-innovation-lion-at-cannes.

6. Amy X. Wang, "Warner Music Group Signs an Algorithm to a
    Record Deal," *Rolling Stone*, March 23, 2019. Accessed at https://
    www.rollingstone.com/pro/news/warner-music-group-endel
    -algorithm-record-deal-811327/.

CHAPTER 6

1. "Google Maps AR," YouTube video, uploaded May 8, 2018, by
    Mandar Limaye. Accessed at https://www.youtube.com/watch?v
    =4F0gFpzsYLM.

2. Ayda Ayoubi, "IKEA Launches Augmented Reality Application,"
    Architect, September 21, 2017. Accessed at https://www
    .architectmagazine.com/technology/ikea-launches-augmented
    -reality-application_0.

3. Cheryl Rosen, "Marriott Debuts Augmented Reality Views of
    Properties on iPhone," Travel Market Report, June 20, 2018.
    Accessed at https://www.travelmarketreport.com/articles
    /Marriott-Debuts-Augmented-Reality-Views-of-Properties-on
    -iPhone.

4. Sarah Perez, "Over a Quarter of U.S. Adults Now Own a Smart
    Speaker, Typically an Amazon Echo," TechCrunch, March 8, 2019.
    Accessed at https://techcrunch.com/2019/03/08/over-a-quarter-of
    -u-s-adults-now-own-a-smart-speaker-typically-an-amazon-echo/.

5. Greg Sterling, "Report: Amazon Internal Data Suggest 'Voice
    Commerce' Virtually Nonexistent," Marketing Land, August 8,
    2018. Accessed at https://marketingland.com/report-amazon
    -internal-data-suggest-voice-commerce-virtually-nonexistent
    -245664.

6. Mary Jo Foley, "Microsoft's Latest Holoportation Demo Shows Off
    Its Mixed Reality, AI, Translation Technologies," ZDNet, July 17,
    2019. Accessed at https://www.zdnet.com/article/microsofts-latest

-holoportation-demo-shows-off-its-mixed-reality-ai-translation
-technologies/.

7. "It's All on Your Fridge," Samsung webpage. Accessed at https://
www.samsung.com/us/explore/family-hub-refrigerator/overview/.

CHAPTER 7

1. Lara O'Reilly, "Bombshell Report Claims U.S. Ad Agencies Unethi-
cally Pad Their Profits with Secret Rebate Schemes," Business
Insider, June 7, 2016. Accessed at https://www.businessinsider.
com/ana-report-alleges-widespread-ad-agency-kickback
-schemes-2016-6.

2. Laurie Sullivan, "Data Estimates 40% of All Media Spend Is
Wasted—How One Company Is Plugging the Holes." Accessed at
https://www.mediapost.com/publications/article/340946/data
-estimates-40-of-all-media-spend-is-wasted-.html.

3. Matt Marshall, "IBM-Unilever Blockchain Pilot Cuts Wasteful Ad
Spend," Venture Beat, August 15, 2019. Accessed at https://
venturebeat.com/2019/08/15/ibm-unilever-blockchain-pilot-cuts
-wasteful-ad-spend/.

CHAPTER 8

1. Ismail Serageldin, "Ancient Alexandria and the Dawn of Medical
Science," National Center for Biotechnology Information,
December 30, 2014. Accessed at https://www.ncbi.nlm.nih.gov
/pmc/articles/PMC3991212/.

2. Joe Dawson, "Who Is That? The Study of Anonymity and Behavior,"
Observer, Association for Psychological Science, March 30, 2018.
Accessed at https://www.psychologicalscience.org/observer/who
-is-that-the-study-of-anonymity-and-behavior.

CHAPTER 9

1. Iris Hearn, "What Mastercard Is Teaching Marketers about Sonic
Branding," Impact, February 13, 2019. Accessed at https://www
.impactbnd.com/blog/mastercard-sonic-branding.

2.   Mark Wilson, " Mastercard Just Launched a Sonic Logo. Here's What It Sounds Like," *Fast Company*, February 13, 2019. Accessed at https://www.fastcompany.com/90305949/mastercard-just-launched-a-sonic-logo-heres-what-it-sounds-like.

3.   Tim Nudd, "Hear Mastercard's New Brand Melody in Various Apps, Styles and Places," Muse by Clio, February 13, 2019. Accessed at https://musebycl.io/music/hear-mastercards-new-brand-melody-various-apps-styles-and-places.

4.   Allen Adamson, "Mastercard's Smart New Branding Strategy Speaks Louder Than Words," *Forbes*, January 7, 2019. Accessed at https://www.forbes.com/sites/allenadamson/2019/01/07/mastercards-smart-new-branding-strategy-speaks-louder-than-words/#ea332b65dbcd.

5.   "Merry Go Round," YouTube video, uploaded January 7, 2020 by Mastercard. Accessed at https://www.youtube.com/watch?v=LMrbsUDp9ts.

6.   "AMP Releases Best Audio Brands 2020 Ranking," press release, AMP, April 14, 2020. Accessed at https://ampsoundbranding.com/best-audio-brands-2020-press-release/.

7.   Blog post, The Marketing Society. Accessed at https://www.marketingsociety.com/the-library/dining-atop-billboard-mastercard.

8.   Lindsey Stein, "Mastercard Impresses with New NYC Culinary Experiences," Campaign US, July 30, 2019. Accessed at https://www.campaignlive.com/article/mastercard-impresses-new-nyc-culinary-experiences/1592396.

9.   Barry Levine, "Mastercard Adds Taste to Brand's Positioning with Custom Macarons," Marketing Dive, September 24, 2019. Accessed at https://www.marketingdive.com/news/mastercard-adds-taste-to-brands-positioning-with-custom-macarons/563552/.

10.   Andrea Cheng, "How a Hotel Gets Its Signature Scent," *Conde Nast Traveler*, August 2, 2019. Accessed at https://www.cntraveler.com/story/how-a-hotel-gets-its-signature-scent.

11.   "The Smell of Commerce: How Companies Use Scents to Sell Their Products," Independent.co.uk. Accessed at https://www.independent.co.uk/news/media/advertising/the-smell-of-commerce-how-companies-use-scents-to-sell-their-products-2338142.html.

CHAPTER 10

1. William Park, "Why We Need to Talk about Cheating," BBC Future, June 25, 2019. Accessed at https://www.bbc.com/future /article/20190625-why-we-need-to-talk-about-cheating.

2. James Surowiecki, "Twilight of the Brands," *New Yorker*, February 10, 2014. Accessed at https://www.newyorker.com/magazine /2014/02/17/twilight-brands.

CHAPTER 11

1. Kevin McSpadden, "You Now Have a Shorter Attention Span Than a Goldfish," *Time*, May 14, 2015. Accessed at https://time.com /3858309/attention-spans-goldfish/.

2. Ryan Holmes, "We Now See 5,000 Ads a Day . . . And It's Getting Worse," LinkedIn, February 19, 2019. Accessed at https://www .linkedin.com/pulse/have-we-reached-peak-ad-social-media-ryan -holmes/.

3. Bryan Clark, "More Than 600 Million Devices Worldwide Are Now Using Ad-Blockers," The Next Web, February 6, 2017. Accessed at https://thenextweb.com/media/2017/02/07/more-than-600 -million-devices-worldwide-are-now-using-ad-blockers/.

4. "Is Ad Blocking Past 2 Billion Worldwide?" Doc Searls Weblog, March 23, 2019. Accessed at https://blogs.harvard.edu/doc /2019/03/23/2billion/.

5. Manish Singh, "Samsung's Preloaded Browser for Android Gets Ad-Blocking Support," Gadgets 360, February 1, 2016. Accessed at https://gadgets.ndtv.com/apps/news/samsungs-preloaded-browser -for-android-gets-ad-blocking-support-796827.

6. Paige Cooper, "43 Social Media Advertising Statistices That Matter to Marketers in 2020," Hootsuite, April 23, 2020. Accessed at https:// blog.hootsuite.com/social-media-advertising-stats/.

7. Roberto Garvin, "How Social Networks Influence 74% of Shoppers for Their Purchasing Decisions Today," Awario, May 11, 2019. Accessed at https://awario.com/blog/how-social-networks -influence-74-of-shoppers-for-their-purchasing-decisions-today/.

8. "A Night with Mona Lisa," Airbnb Newsroom. Accessed at https:// news.airbnb.com/louvre/.

9. "Brandz Top 100 Most Valuable Global Brands 2020," Brandz.

Accessed at https://www.brandz.com/admin/uploads/files/2020
_BrandZ_Global_Top_100_Report.pdf.

CHAPTER 12

1. Jennifer Faull, "Brands Form 'Voice Coalition' to Prep for Alexa and
    Siri Changing the Way We Shop," Drum, June 19, 2019. Accessed
    at https://www.thedrum.com/news/2019/06/19/brands-form-voice
    -coalition-prep-alexa-and-siri-changing-the-way-we-shop.

CHAPTER 14

1. Carolyn Harding, "Instagram's Live Donation Feature: Just the
    Facts," Digital Media Solutions, May 4, 2020. Accessed at https://
    insights.digitalmediasolutions.com/news/instagram-live
    -donations.

CHAPTER 15

1. "Leadership Series: Purpose-Driven Leadership," EY. Accessed at
    https://www.ey.com/Publication/vwLUAssets/ey-purpose-driven
    -leadership/$File/ey-purpose-driven-leadership.pdf.
2. Robert E. Quinn and Anjan V. Thakor, "Creating a Purpose-Driven
    Organization," Harvard Business Review, July–August, 2018. Accessed
    at https://hbr.org/2018/07/creating-a-purpose-driven-organization.
3. "The Economic Graph Research CFP," LinkedIn Economic Graph
    Research. Accessed at https://engineering.linkedin.com/teams
    /data/projects/economic-graph-research.
4. "Two-Thirds of Consumers Worldwide Now Buy on Beliefs,"
    Edelman, October 2, 2018. Accessed at https://www.edelman.com
    /news-awards/two-thirds-consumers-worldwide-now-buy
    -beliefs#:~:text=Nearly%20two%2Dthirds%20(64%20percent,13%20
    points%20from%20last%20year.
5. Zameena Mejia, "Nearly 9 Out of 10 Millennials Would Consider
    Taking a Pay Cut to Get This," CNBC, June 28, 2018. Accessed at
    https://www.cnbc.com/2018/06/27/nearly-9-out-of-10-millennials
    -would-consider-a-pay-cut-to-get-this.html.

CHAPTER 16

1.   "2019 Edelman Trust Barometer Special Report: In Brands We Trust?" Edelman. Accessed at https://www.edelman.com/sites/g /files/aatuss191/files/2019-07/2019_edelman_trust_barometer _special_report_in_brands_we_trust.pdf.

2.   The World's Most Ethical Companies homepage. Accessed at https://www.worldsmostethicalcompanies.com.

3.   Janika Parmar, "'Ethical Consumers'—Why CP Companies Need to Act Fast," Capgemini, April 3, 2019. Accessed at https://www .capgemini.com/us-en/2019/04/ethical-consumers-why-cp -companies-need-to-act-fast/.

4.   "WFA Launches World's First Guide on Data Ethics for Brands," press release, World Federation of Advertisers, June 1, 2020. Accessed at https://wfanet.org/knowledge/item/2020/06/01/WFA -launches-worlds-first-guide-on-data-ethics-for-brands.

5.   "FIXD—Never Get Ripped Off by Mechanics Again," YouTube video, uploaded April 28, 2017. Accessed at https://youtu.be /jDasRRpmWZo.

6.   "Media Transparency Initiative: K2 Report," ANA, press release. Accessed at https://www.ana.net/content/show/id/industry -initiative-media-transparency-report.

7.   Paul Nicholson, "Global Sports Sponsorship Spend to Drop by 37% to $28.9bn, Says Report," Inside World Football, May 18, 2020. Accessed at http://www.insideworldfootball.com/2020/05/18 /global-sports-sponsorship-spend-drop-37-28-9bn-says-report/.

8.   "Corruption in Sport," Interpol crimes webpage. Accessed at https://www.interpol.int/en/Crimes/Corruption/Corruption-in -sport.

Index

About the Author

Raja Rajamannar is the chief marketing and communications officer of Mastercard and is also the president of the company's healthcare business. He is an accomplished global executive with more than three decades of experience, living and working in various parts of the world.

Raja is globally recognized as a highly innovative and transformational leader, and has received numerous accolades over the years. To name a few, he has been listed as one of the World's Most Influential CMOs by *Forbes*, one of the Most Innovative CMOs in the World by *Business Insider*, and as one of the most tech-savvy CMOs by *Adweek*. Raja has been named as the 2018 World Federation of Advertisers Global Marketer of the Year and the 2019 ANA Educational Foundation Marketer of the Year. He is an inductee to the CMO Hall of Fame by the CMO Club. Raja also serves as the president of the World Federation of Advertisers.

At Mastercard, Raja is responsible for successfully leading the company's marketing transformation, including the integration of the marketing and communication functions, the development of Priceless experiential platforms, and the creation and deployment of cutting-edge, marketing-led business models into the core of the company. Raja has overseen the successful evolution of Mastercard's identity for the digital age, pioneering Mastercard's move to become a symbol brand and launching its breakthrough sonic brand platform. Under Raja's stewardship, the Mastercard brand made significant strides. Interbrand ranked Mastercard as the fastest-growing brand across all industries and categories worldwide in 2019. And in 2020, Mastercard became a top 10 brand globally in BrandZ rankings.

Raja spent half his career managing businesses and the other half managing marketing. He has been recognized for driving business transformation across a variety of industries and geographies, including consumer-packaged goods, financial services, and healthcare. Prior to Mastercard, he served as chief transformation officer of the health insurance firm Anthem (formerly WellPoint) and served as chief innovation and marketing officer of Humana. Earlier in his career, Raja held various senior management roles with Citibank, including chairman and CEO of Diners Club North America. Prior to Citi, Raja worked at Unilever in India, where he got his sales and marketing foundations. He started his working career in India with Asian Paints.

Raja is a member of the Board of Directors of PPL Corporation, a US Fortune 500 company, and Bon Secours Mercy Health, a not-for-profit hospital system in the US and Ireland.

Raja graduated in chemical engineering from the College of Technology at Osmania University and did his postgraduate work at the Indian Institute of Management, Bangalore.

Raja is an animal lover, especially of dogs. He is a vegan and a longtime practitioner of yoga and meditation.